A HOLE IN THE FENCE

David Foley

A HOLE IN THE FENCE

OBERON BOOKS
LONDON

First published in 2007 by Oberon Books Ltd
521 Caledonian Road, London N7 9RH
Tel: 020 7607 3637 / Fax: 020 7607 3629
e-mail: info@oberonbooks.com
www.oberonbooks.com

A catalogue record for this book is available from the British
Library.

Cover design by Oberon Books

ISBN: 1 84002 790 8 / 978-1-84002-790-7

Printed in Great Britain by Antony Rowe Ltd, Chippenham.

Characters

THE PROFESSOR

JAMIE

THEO

MR VOLE

REVEREND HUTCH

The Fairies

PETEY

ELLA

CHUCK

The Decoys

GEORGE

MICK

VERN

The following characters are played by other characters:
Dr Cranky, Policeman, Military Police, Mr Pumphrey,
Mr Haney, Mr Chump, Prison Guard, Roosevelt, his
Aide, Bishop Woollett, Senators

Set
The set is a bare stage. All settings are suggested with a
couple of tables, a few chairs, perhaps a step ladder or
two. Oh, and a bed.

A Hole in the Fence was first performed at the White Bear Theatre, London, in a productions by Box of Tricks Theatre Company, in association with Joabri Productions Ltd and the White Bear Theatre Club on 19 June 2007, with the following cast:

THEO Henry Maynard
JAMIE Domenico Listorti
THE PROFESSOR Edward Grace
REVEREND HUTCH Adam Price
ELLA Andy Egwuatu
CHUCK Pedro Reichert
PETEY Mark Collier
MICK Arthur Wilson
VERN Nathan Cable
GEORGE Ian Stopford
MR VOLE Peter Leafe

Directors Adam Quayle and Hannah Tyrrell-Pinder
Designer Georgia Lowe
Lighting Designer Lawrence Stromski
Sound Designers Chris James and Mat Williams
Costume Designer Victoria Povey

A Hole in the Fence is based on a scandal that occurred in Newport, Rhode Island, in 1919. For research and material from court transcripts, I am indebted to Lawrence R. Murphy's account in *Perverts by Official Order*. Coincidentally, at more or less the same time, the American playwright Thornton Wilder, then unknown, stayed at the Army and Navy YMCA in Newport, working on his first novel. His involvement in the scandal, however, is entirely imaginary.

Act I

An empty stage. The PROFESSOR *appears center stage. He is of an indeterminate age—strictly speaking in his twenties, but one of those people who, owing perhaps to a receding hairline, a mustache, a little paunchiness, or just a certain premature maturity, never look—have never looked—young. He wears a tweed coat and a pair of baggy trousers, both slightly shabby. He speaks to the audience with nervous enthusiasm.*

PROFESSOR: Good evening, good evening! And welcome to the [XX] Theatre, where tonight's— Shall we call it an 'entertainment'? Let's.— Where tonight's entertainment will be *A Hole in the Fence* by David Foley, directed by [XX], with the invaluable participation of [XX], [XX] (*Etc. Checks a notecard he is holding.*) Did I get everybody? Did I mention [XX]? (*Calls offstage.*) Shall I do lights and costumes? Hm? (*No answer; to audience.*) Oh, well, never mind. (*Shoves the notecard absently into his pocket; then, shading his eyes against the lights:*) Everybody comfortable? Good, good!

Now! To begin with, you must imagine that this bare stage— (*Glancing anxiously into the wings.*) which we hope won't be bare much longer—is the seaside town of Newport, Rhode Island. Here, when the republic was young, women paced the rocky cliffs waiting for whaling ships to return from the sea. Here the wealth to be got from blubber and sperm raised a prosperous New England community. Here, too, at the end of the last century those barons of steel and oil and rail raised their baronial mansions. Here the 'season', when it had worn out its yearly welcome in New York, took its glittering baggage; and took it, you may imagine, in carriages crammed with silken dresses and morning coats and canes with burnished gold knobs.

Now, however, it is 1919. The Naval base here—established in 1882—has expanded boisterously with the recent war. Young men from all walks of life, having left their paternal homes with fresh faces and naive expectations, crowd the streets; are invited to afternoon teas by the daughters of Newport; attend musicales sponsored by the city fathers;

are visited by clergy of the various denominations that this exceptionally tolerant town encompasses; participate in any number of wholesome recreations devised to make them less bewildered and homesick so far away from familiar things…

No place, of course, is more important to a young man far from home than the YMCA. Built in 1911 with a $315,000 gift from Mrs Thomas Emery of Cincinnati, Ohio, and located right next door to the county courthouse, the Army and Navy Young Men's Christian Association of Newport, Rhode Island, was conceived as a place where the moral health of these young sailors could be attended to. It had everything a boy could need: a restaurant, a barber shop, a gymnasium, a large lobby for meeting and socializing, small rooms upstairs which could be rented cheaply for the night. Oh, yes, and it had a billiard room. (*Calls offstage.*) Ready? (*To audience.*) Scene one.

As the PROFESSOR exits, JAMIE and THEO enter, carrying pool cues. JAMIE is a sinewy, effeminate man in his early twenties. THEO is taller, strapping, slightly menacing. Both wear sailor shirts and hats and jeans. They mime playing pool.

JAMIE: Six ball in the corner pocket.

CHUCK appears in back of them, holding two pool balls, which he smacks together.

THEO: Sharp.

JAMIE shrugs and moves to another position at the table, brushing lightly against THEO as he goes.

JAMIE: Four in the side. (*He aims and shoots. CHUCK smacks his pool balls together. JAMIE walks by THEO again, very close.*) Two in the side. (*Same business.*)

THEO: (*Sarcastically.*) Awwwwww.

JAMIE: (*Meets his gaze a moment.*) Pity.

THEO: (*Chalking up.*) Where's your berth?

JAMIE: I work in the dispensary.

THEO: (*Interested.*) Yeah? (*Lowers his voice.*) Can you get stuff?

JAMIE: What's in it for me?

Pause. They look at each other. THEO breaks first and moves away, positioning himself for his shot.

THEO: I got cash.

JAMIE: (*Uninterested.*) Oh.

At JAMIE's tone, THEO hesitates. Then:

THEO: Seven in the corner. (*He does it.*)

JAMIE: Brilliant. (*THEO positions himself for his next shot. JAMIE passes behind him and gazes at his butt. He lets the pool cue trail across it.*) Mmmmmm.

THEO whirls on him and grabs him by the shirt.

THEO: HEY! (*He holds him for a moment as they look at each other. Menacingly:*) Do you know what I could do to you?

JAMIE: (*Returning his gaze; coolly.*) Uh-huh.

VERN, a slightly stupid, red-haired sailor, appears downstage left. JAMIE's gaze shifts to him. VERN sends a few hesitant glances back in his direction.

(*Appreciatively.*) Well, will ya lookit that…

THEO glances over his shoulder and sees VERN. Turning back to JAMIE, he puts his hand up and forces JAMIE's gaze back to meet his.

THEO: Hey. I thought we had a game on.

JAMIE: (*Beat.*) All right.

They continue their game, but each movement becomes laden with intent, a tango of suspicion and desire. PETEY appears downstage right. He is a young sailor who gives the impression of still having a bit of baby fat on him. His hair is very blond, his face is very round, his eyes are very blue. His expression manages to combine both innocence and perpetual horniness.

He crosses the stage rapidly, whistling to himself, sees VERN *as he is about to pass him, stops baldly, swivels, takes a few steps in the direction he came from, fixes* VERN *with a sidelong gaze.* VERN *casts a few nervous glances in his direction. Abruptly* PETEY *approaches him.*

PETEY: Say, got a cigarette?

Without saying anything, VERN *takes out a pack and proffers it to* PETEY. PETEY *takes one, puts it in his mouth, then pats his pockets.*

No light.

As VERN *lights* PETEY's *cigarette,* PETEY *reaches up and steadies his hand.*

Thanks, mate. (*Beat.*) Saturday night, huh? You got somethin' on.

VERN: Nope.

PETEY: Me neither. Nothin' to do in this one-horse town. And I'm about as horny as a monkey in a fishhouse. Know what I'm sayin'. But what can you do? Birds here won't give you the time of day. 'Less you got the dough. It's a rich man's world, huh? What're you up to?

VERN: Just—um—just standin' here.

PETEY: (*Beat.*) Well, that's it, isn't it? All you can do. Just stand here. I never seen a place as dull as this one. (*Grabs his crotch.*) Oh, but, say, I could use some tonight. I'm like to explode right here. What about you?

VERN: Um…

PETEY: But what's a fella to do? Not a bird in sight, right? Even if they was, isn't one of 'em would spit on you to stop you dyin' a thirst. What's a fella to do? What, what, what?

VERN: Dunno.

PETEY: Drown your sorrows. Tell you what. I got some hooch on me. Bet you could use a snort.

VERN: (*Confused.*) A snort?

PETEY: Some of the hard stuff. (*VERN's eyes widen.*) Not here, though. People watching. Tell you what. I got a room here for the night. Go up there, shall we?

VERN: (*Swallowing nervously.*) OK.

PETEY: Well, come on then!

He drags VERN offstage. GEORGE and MICK roll the bed on stage. The bed now represents two different rooms at the Y, where two assignations are going on. JAMIE and THEO give their pool cues to CHUCK as they enter the 'room'.

THEO: This your room?

JAMIE: I rent it weekends sometimes. You never know. Like it?

THEO: What's to like?

JAMIE: (*Goes up to THEO and strokes his chest.*) You tell me.

He puts his hand on THEO's cheek and makes as if to kiss him. THEO grabs his wrist and holds it away from his face.

THEO: None o' that.

JAMIE: Suit yourself.

VERN and PETEY appear and sit on the edge of the bed. They pass a flask back and forth.

PETEY: You're a funny guy. Don't say much. It's the quiet ones you gotta watch out for. Always full-a surprises. I bet you're *full* of surprises. Am I right?

He squeezes VERN's thigh. VERN looks at his hand with dumb apprehension.

THEO: Have you got anything?

JAMIE: Any what?

VERN grabs the flask and takes a long swig.

THEO: You know.

PETEY: Whoa! Save some o' that for me!

JAMIE takes a small paper packet from his pocket and offers it to THEO. THEO opens it, sniffs some. He shoves the packet in his pocket.

JAMIE: Hey!

THEO: You can get more.

They study each other warily. PETEY stands and stretches.

PETEY: God, but I'm horny! Show you something.

He turns upstage and drops his trousers. VERN's jaw drops. JAMIE sits on the edge of the bed.

Scared a lotta birds with that. Touch it if you like.

VERN just stares, dumbfounded.

Aw, come on!

He throws himself on VERN with athletic enthusiasm. THEO starts to undo his belt.

THEO: All right. Do it now.

All four of them exit. The PROFESSOR and MR VOLE appear, each with a chair. They place them opposite each other. The PROFESSOR sits and lays a napkin over his lap and pulls out a book which he reads as he mimes eating his breakfast. MR VOLE is a short, wiry man, about forty, with a face like an axe and sharp, narrow eyes.

MR VOLE: Ah, Professor! Good morning! Your morning repast?

PROFESSOR: Good morning, Mr Vole! Yes, a little late, I'm afraid. I'm never as matutinal as I would like. Discipline, as always, eludes me. These late nights…

MR VOLE: But you see! I haven't eaten yet either. Shall I join you, then?

PROFESSOR: I'd be honored.

MR VOLE sits and tucks a napkin into his collar.

MR VOLE: You keep late hours?

PROFESSOR: Hm?

MR VOLE: You said you were up late. The writer's life, I
imagine. Burning the midnight oil. Scribbling away.

PROFESSOR: Alas, no. I was enjoying the conviviality of some
young sailors here at the Y.

MR VOLE: (*Attentively.*) Were you, then?

PROFESSOR: Yes. My head… (*He taps it woefully.*)

MR VOLE: Oh, I see. Taking of the grape.

PROFESSOR: The grain, I must confess.

MR VOLE: (*Shaking his head good-humoredly.*) Tut-tut-tut. (*Beat.*) I
bet you see a lot.

PROFESSOR: A lot of what?

MR VOLE: Come now, Professor. You're a writer. Not much gets
by *you.*

PROFESSOR: I try to keep my eyes open. And my heart.

*At this moment ELLA approaches the table. He's a black man
of about thirty, with a lissome walk and a little liner around
the eyes.*

ELLA: (*To MR VOLE.*) What'll it be, dearie?

MR VOLE: Two over easy. Bacon. Don't burn the toast.

ELLA goes. MR VOLE leans closer to the PROFESSOR.

You see that?

PROFESSOR: What?

MR VOLE: Cosmetics! Eyebrow pencil! I can spot 'em a mile
off.

PROFESSOR: Spot what a mile off?

*MR VOLE leans back and gazes speculatively at the PROFESSOR
a moment.*

MR VOLE: Professor, you are either the greatest innocent alive
or the greatest dissembler.

PROFESSOR: I hope that I am both, Mr Vole.

MR VOLE: Both?

PROFESSOR: It needs both to write.

MR VOLE: (*Laughs.*) You're an original, you are! (*Leans closer.*) No, I'll tell you what I mean, 'cause I've got a notion you could help me. I mean *perverts*!

PROFESSOR: Perverts?

MR VOLE: Now, you're not that innocent, Professor. This place is jammed with 'em. I know. I make it my business to know perverts.

PROFESSOR: (*Curiously.*) Your *business*? How extraordinary.

ELLA enters with an invisible plate of food and a very real and visibly steaming pot of coffee. He mimes putting the plate in front of MR VOLE, then tilts the coffee-pot which, since there's no table, hovers alarmingly over MR VOLE's lap.

ELLA: Coffee?

MR VOLE: NO! Thank you. (*She goes. MR VOLE leans forward.*) I've heard things that'd curl your hair. They tell me things. The things I've heard. Orgies. Men dressed up in women's clothes. Drugs. Unnatural acts. Things I wouldn't repeat to a decent man like yourself.

PROFESSOR: And yet they've told them to you.

MR VOLE: I got ways. Did I ever tell you what I did before I joined the Navy?

PROFESSOR: I don't believe so.

MR VOLE: I was nine years a detective for the Connecticut State Police.

PROFESSOR: Goodness! Well, from now on I shall be on my best behavior around you.

MR VOLE: Not in the least, Professor. I recognize in you a fellow spirit. One who, like myself, hates vice and loves virtue.

PROFESSOR: It was the Greek ideal.

MR VOLE: (*Suspiciously.*) If you say so, Professor. If you say so. But you keep your eyes open and you'll see what I mean. And I'll let slip something: I've got something on. I can't talk about it now. Top secret. But you wait a bit. This town is gonna see a thing or two.

PROFESSOR: Every sense in my body, Mr Vole, has been alerted.

MR VOLE: (*Smiles; beat.*) Well, sir. I owe you thanks. It's not often I get a chance to chat with an educated man. How does your work progress?

PROFESSOR: Fitfully, I'm afraid.

MR VOLE: You keep at it. I can see you're a man of real understanding. (*Wipes his mouth.*) You know, I once thought of trying something in that line myself.

PROFESSOR: Writing?

MR VOLE: Believe it or don't. What got me thinking about it was the detective work. You have to know what makes people tick. What deep down inside motivates them. Same with writing, I reckon.

PROFESSOR: Yes, but the hardest motives to understand, Mr Vole, are one's own.

MR VOLE: (*Looks at him sharply again.*) If you say so, Professor. If you say so.

The PROFESSOR crosses downstage and addresses the audience.

PROFESSOR: I feel I owe the audience an explanation for my own involvement in this affair. Mr Vole has let slip that I was writing, and indeed I was, preparing the first of those literary works which have since earned me my modest fame.

I was young and poor, and the only garret my meager finances could afford was a little room at the top of the YMCA. There my scribbling earned me a reputation for 'book-larnin'' among the other denizens, awed or puzzled as they were by the mysterious communion of pen and paper. Professor is what they called me then, and Professor, for the next two hours, is what I prefer to call myself. Now then! (*Calls offstage.*) Mr Vole?

He exits right and MR VOLE marches on left, followed by the three Decoys. They stand in formation in front of him, backs to the audience, as he addresses them.

MR VOLE: You all know why you're here. Each man among you has been recommended as a sailor of upstanding character, moral correctness, and devotion to the service of the Navy.

Pause. He takes a solemn breath.

Gentlemen, we stand upon a sink of vice such as would make a Roman emperor blush. Do you know what vice is, gentlemen? It's a disease. Allow it a purchase and it will spread, infecting the healthy and debilitating the body of the state itself. Every mother sends her boy to the Navy hoping we'll send her back a man, a man trained in the highest ideals of the republic. Well, every mother's son here is in danger: in danger of infection from this gross, disfiguring disease. The solemn duty we take upon ourselves today, the solemn oath we make to that faraway mother pining for her boy, is to strain every sinew in our bodies, expend every ounce of our courage, to root out this pernicious plague.

Your duty, to put it plainly, is to obtain information about and evidence against the cocksuckers and rectum receivers who are plying their infamous trade in the very bowels of the United States Navy. To do this you must enter the dens of vice itself. You must pretend to be one of them, make free with them, be jolly and good-natured, make assignations, and allow yourselves to be taken into their confidence.

Every morning before ten hundred hours, you will submit a report typed in quadruplicate. Reports should be detailed and frank and should include the names and ranks of each suspect as well as where they live and where they are stationed.

Is there anyone now who wishes to be dismissed from these duties?

No one moves.

Brave men! I leave you with these three words: Infiltrate. Penetrate. Report.

Dismissed.

He salutes. They salute back and begin to leave.

Tetchill!

VERN stops and turns back.

VERN: Sir?

MR VOLE: Come into my office and be debriefed.

VERN: (*Shocked.*) *Sir*!

MR VOLE: And make your *report*, Tetchill.

VERN: Yes, sir.

They step into MR VOLE's 'office'.

MR VOLE: Proceed.

Note: any temptation to show MR VOLE taking a lascivious interest in VERN's report should be resisted. Whatever subterranean motives might underlie his actions, his conduct should always be that of a self-convicted enemy of vice.

VERN: Suspect accosted—

MR VOLE: Name, Tetchill!

VERN: Vern Tetchill, sir.

MR VOLE: Name of the *suspect*.

VERN: Petey Corker, sir.

MR VOLE: Proceed.

VERN: Suspect accosted me in the lobby of the YMCA. After a brief conversation, suspect invited me to his room. On reaching his room, suspect gave me whiskey, and laid his hand on my knee. He kissed me several minutes, then pulled my penis from my trousers and sucked thereon until there was emission. After spitting in the chamber pot, he offered to kiss me again, but I made an excuse and left.

MR VOLE: The report. (*VERN produces a sheet of paper from his pocket and hands it to MR VOLE.*) Good work, Tetchill. Keep it up.

They exit separately as the PROFESSOR enters with JAMIE.

PROFESSOR: If the audience will forgive another intrusion, it occurs to me that there are certain technical matters that require explanation but which lie, alas, outside my own area of expertise. I will then briefly turn the program over to James Peacock who will elucidate a few minor points. Mr Peacock.

As JAMIE assumes center stage, the Fairies rush on downstage with cries of, 'Tell 'em about it, Jamie!' 'Go it, girl!' 'Let the Duchess speak!' etc. JAMIE addresses the audience.

JAMIE: The Professor wanted me to say a few words about Fairies. First thing you gotta know is a Fairy ain't just a Fairy. Call 'er a Fairy, call 'er a queer, call 'er a queen. But a Fairy ain't just a Fairy. You got three types. There's your pogues, your cocksuckers, and your two-way artists. Now Ella here's a pogue. (*ELLA bows.*) She takes it up the ass. That's all. She won't take nothin' in her mouth. Don't even try.

Chuck, she's a cocksucker. No explanation needed. Petey's a two-way artist. Turn her up, turn her down, turn her over. It's all the same to Petey. Versatile, I think you call it. Them's the Fairies.

Cries of protest from the Fairies: 'What about you, Madame Thing?' etc.

Quiet! A girl's gotta have a few secrets.

Then there's Trade.

THEO enters and takes up a position downstage, apart from the Fairies. He lights a cigarette.

First you gotta know what Trade ain't. Trade ain't a Fairy and Trade ain't queer. And Trade don't suck and Trade don't get fucked. (*He looks at THEO with a certain bitterness.*) But if you're nice to Trade and you give him pretty presents, he might just be nice to you in return. I think you know what I mean. (*He turns away from THEO.*) There's Trade that stays with the same Fairy all their lives, keeping house and making nice. But Trade ain't queer. That's the difference.

As the others leave the stage:

It's a different world, ain't it, ladies and gentlemen, lying just beneath the surface of your own? Where did you think it all ran down to, all that dirty stuff you try to wash away? It's right here, right where you can get at it when you want it, when things are a little too clean where you live and you want to get out and get away and muck it up a bit.

The REVEREND HUTCH enters, a bespectacled man in his early forties wearing the collar of an Episcopal priest. He appears to be in a hurry.

Ain't that right, Reverend?

REVEREND: (*Stops, blinks.*) Hm? What? Why, Jamie? How do you do?

JAMIE: Scrumptious, Revvy dear. And yourself?

REVEREND: (*Uncertainly.*) Oh, you know. Fine, fine. Occupied. The life of a Navy chaplain...

JAMIE: I know, I know. 'A man he works from sun to sun, but...'

REVEREND: (*Vaguely.*) Quite, quite.

JAMIE: Rushing off?

REVEREND: A young man, in need of spiritual comfort.

JAMIE: That so? Well, don't let me keep you.

REVEREND: Yes… Yes… Must… Good-bye.

He starts off.

JAMIE: Oh, Reverend! (*The REVEREND stops.*) Give him some extra comfort for me.

The REVEREND blinks, blushes, starts to say something, then hurries offstage. JAMIE smiles after him, then notices THEO, still loitering downstage, smoking.

Hey, sailor. Thought I might've seen you around.

THEO: I been around.

JAMIE: Aw. Just my luck. I missed ya. (*THEO shrugs.*) Aren't you cold standing out here in the street?

THEO: I'm OK.

JAMIE: It's warmer in my room. Whyn't you come over?

THEO: (*Without looking at him.*) Have you got the stuff?

JAMIE: (*Wearily.*) Yeah, I got the stuff. (*THEO doesn't move.*) Well, suit yourself. I ain't begging. They's guys all over town happy to share what I got.

He crosses away, then stops and looks back at THEO. THEO casts a wary glance up and down the street. Then he tosses his cigarette and follows JAMIE offstage at a safe distance. CHUCK appears downstage, a tall, rangy man with dark hair. He is something of an operator with a quick, easy patter and a high-strung energy. GEORGE enters: stocky, surly, bull-headed. The following assignations occur in different places, but the bed, of course, should be used freely.

CHUCK: I thought you mightn't come.

GEORGE: Said I would.

CHUCK: I been stood up before. Twice just last week. Same guy.

GEORGE: Well… I said I'd come and I did.

CHUCK: Then ain't you a peach!

He puts his hand on GEORGE's shoulder and rubs it. GEORGE submits stiffly.

GEORGE: When's the movie?

CHUCK: Oh, we got time. Let's say we take a walk, eh? Up on the Cliff Walk. Beautiful night for it. We can watch the submarines race.

GEORGE: Whatever you say.

They start to walk.

CHUCK: I can tell you're the romantic type. (*GEORGE shrugs.*) Strong and silent, that's it. This looks like a likely spot.

He tries to kiss him. GEORGE turns his head away.

All right. We can skip the formalities.

As he drops to his knees, the stage goes dark except for a tight spot on GEORGE's face as he makes his report.

GEORGE: I agreed to meet the suspect for a movie and, on meeting, he suggested we go to the Cliff Walk, a notorious meeting place for perverts. On coming to a secluded area, suspect drew my tool from my trousers and sucked me off as I stood against a fence. We returned to town too late for the movie.

Spot out on GEORGE. VERN and ELLA appear. ELLA is kissing the sailor tenderly and stroking his face.

ELLA: Such pretty red hair. You're very pretty, you know. If I could have you, I wouldn't need nobody else. Could you do that for me, sugar? If I was true to you, would you be true to me and not go with anyone else?

VERN: Sure.

ELLA: I could do things for you, sugar. I could make you feel good. Doesn't that feel good? Now doesn't it?

Tight spot on VERN's face.

VERN: After loving me up for several minutes and working my penis to a state of rigidity, suspect put cold cream on it and asked me to enter him in the rectum.

Spot out on VERN. PETEY and MICK, a blond Midwestern type, are sitting on the bed, kissing. PETEY places his hand on MICK's crotch, and MICK reacts as if jolted.

PETEY: Whoa, boy! Whoa! Steady on.

As PETEY's head works down towards MICK's crotch, the spot closes in on MICK.

MICK: Suspect placed my cock in his mouth and sucked on it until there was–oh, God–emission.

Lights come up and the Decoys and Fairies scramble to change partners. Now it's GEORGE and ELLA, MICK and CHUCK, and PETEY and VERN.

ELLA: I know you'll leave me just like the others. I bet you got a dozen boys like me. Oh, it don't matter. Just be here for me tonight, sugar. Be here tonight.

He freezes as GEORGE makes his report.

GEORGE: Suspect put vaseline on my tool and invited me to enter him like a woman. After going on for several minutes, I shot a load into his rectum.

CHUCK: (*Moving down MICK's body; MICK is trembling with excitement.*) That's it, kid. Steady as she goes. Nice 'n' easy. (*He yanks MICK's pants down and freezes.*)

MICK: (*Breathlessly.*) He unbuttoned my trousers, pulled out my penis, and sucked same.

VERN is squatting with PETEY's head in his lap.

VERN: When he was done, he took a handkerchief from his pocket and wiped his mouth.

Another scramble. PETEY and GEORGE, ELLA and MICK, and CHUCK and VERN.

GEORGE: I gave him a load and he ate it nicely.

VERN: He spit on the ground and buttoned his trousers.

MICK: We continued on like that until I...uh!...discharged.

The spotlights close in again on all three faces, and we see them each 'come'.

VERN: Ohhhhhhh!

GEORGE: Oh. Oh. Oh. Yeah.

MICK: Oh! Oh! Yes! Oh, God! Yes! Yes!

He looks around, frightened, as if someone may have heard him. Blackout. When the lights come up again, the stage is bare. The PROFESSOR enters.

PROFESSOR: We must once again beg the audience's patience for just a moment and, this time, with some embarrassment. Times, as you know, are hard in the theatre and money is tight. Moreover, we have had a very difficult time with the government agencies who are understandably reluctant to support work they consider immoral. We, of course, have argued that while *parts* of tonight's program may *seem* immoral, the overall moral *tone* is quite serious and quite, I might add, what it should be. So far, however, those holding the strings of purse haven't bought it.

All this weary introduction merely to say that certain exigencies of budget have required us to use the same actor to play several parts. 'Doubling up,' we call it in the theatre. In this scene, for instance, Ella will be playing (*Pulls a notecard from his pocket.*) Dr Emilius Cranky, chairman of the board of directors of the YMCA and a man of the most unyielding moral principles. We apologize for any confusion this may engender.

CHUCK and VERN carry on and place a table on which ELLA, as DR CRANKY, is sitting languorously. MR VOLE enters and sternly faces him. CHUCK and VERN exit.

ELLA wears the suit of a prosperous citizen of 1919, padded to suggest girth. It fits him loosely, like a clown's. A handlebar mustache is pasted haphazardly above his mouth. As the scene opens, he is filing his nails, but he puts the nail file down when he begins to speak.

Note: when anyone in the main cast is required to play another part, it should be as if the character, not the actor, is playing the part, with whatever ease or difficulty might be expected under the circumstances.

ELLA: What you say astonishes me, sir. Every fiber of my being hopes that you are mistaken.

MR VOLE: I can certainly see, Dr Cranky, how shocking this must be to a man of your… (*Tightly.*) decency and high-mindedness, but I can assure you we have uncovered only a fraction of the cesspool seething underneath this city.

ELLA: Your image is very strong, Mr Vole. As regards this… this 'investigation', please excuse the impertinence, but under whose authority do you operate this investigation?

MR VOLE: No impertinence, doctor. My instructions come from the very highest level–from the Secretary of the Navy himself, Mr Franklin Delano Roosevelt!

ELLA: Ah… Miss Roosevelt.

MR VOLE: (*Glares at ELLA for a moment, then shouts.*) Professor!

The PROFESSOR pokes his head in stage right.

He did it again!

PROFESSOR: Ella, please….

ELLA: (*Casually.*) I slipped. I'm sorry. (*To MR VOLE.*) *Do* forgive me.

MR VOLE: If it happens again, I'm leaving the stage.

ELLA: Dear me. How ever will we survive?

PROFESSOR: Gentlemen, please. Continue.

He backs off the stage.

ELLA: Your instructions come directly from… *Mr* Roosevelt?

MR VOLE: I have been assigned to the case by his direct order. Secretary Roosevelt takes, I have been assured, a personal interest in rooting out vice not only in the Navy, but in the area surrounding the naval base.

ELLA: Meaning?

MR VOLE: Meaning, Dr Cranky, that the conditions of vice existing in Newport present a danger to the young men of the Navy and that the Navy, therefore, has a compelling interest in cleaning Newport up!

ELLA: It seems to me, Mr Vole, that such conditions are more peculiar to the Navy than to Newport.

MR VOLE: Begging your pardon, sir, and allowing for the insult to the United States Navy, our investigation has already revealed a most unpleasant scene among the civilians here. There is even (*With sudden viciousness.*) a nigger waiter at your very own YMCA who is a very captain of perversion.

ELLA: (*Stung; with controlled fury.*) I trust, Mr Vole, that there is no employee in my establishment that answers to so intemperate a description and I ask you quickly to make your point clear.

MR VOLE: What if I told you, doctor, that among the most notorious perverts in this town is a reverend of the Episcopal church?

ELLA: I would hope that you were joking, sir, but I would advise you that I fail to see the humor in such a joke.

MR VOLE: I mean it. I've got the evidence. Almost as if I'd seen it with my own eyes. We can shield our eyes from unpleasant facts, Dr Cranky, but they don't go away. Now, you're a man with a certain standing in the community. The Navy can take care of its own, never fear. But we need a man on the civilian side, a man who can engage the cooperation of the local authorities in apprehending those offenders who lie, sadly, outside the Navy's jurisdiction. I'm suggesting, sir, with the deepest respect, that that man is you.

ELLA: Sir, you have shaken me to the bone. If what you say is true, then it is indeed my duty to assist you in any way I can. Perhaps at your earliest convenience, you could present your evidence to me so that I may judge for myself of these matters.

MR VOLE: (*Rising.*) That I will, sir. And it'll singe your eyebrows off.

ELLA: (*Hand to mouth.*) Oooh!

DR CRANKY's office disappears, and the bed at the Y is reassembled. JAMIE and GEORGE enter.

JAMIE: Home sweet home.

GEORGE: You live here?

JAMIE: I *reside* on the base. But that's no home. That's a jail term. Fortunately (*Touches GEORGE's chest.*) I get time off for *bad* behavior.

GEORGE: (*Moving away.*) If you don't like it, why are you there?

JAMIE: A girl's gotta do something. I can't take in sewing and I ain't cut out to be a priest. What's a poor boy to do?

GEORGE: (*Suddenly.*) The Navy ain't for men like you!

JAMIE: (*Suspiciously.*) What? Oh, Lord. Not this. I'm a dirty pervert, am I? I'm a sick queen. You think I ain't heard it before. Well, what are you here for, sailor? Couldn't get a woman tonight? If you can't get a woman to give you a two dollar blowjob in this town, you ain't half trying. I can give you some names if you want. No? Then keep a lid on it. If you want it, sailor, spare me the chatter. If you don't, get lost.

GEORGE: I didn't mean no offense.

JAMIE: (*Beat; laughs bitterly.*) Oh, none taken, dearie, none taken. (*Sits on the bed.*) Come over here now. Let's get cozy. (*GEORGE sits down stiffly beside him. JAMIE starts to unbutton GEORGE's shirt.*) Now, what kind of man would you say the Navy's for?

GEORGE: Hey! I said no offense.

JAMIE: And I said none taken. I was just wondering (*Rubbing GEORGE's chest.*) if *you* was the kind of man the Navy's made for.

GEORGE: (*Uncomfortably.*) I thought you wanted to cut the chat.

JAMIE: Suits me.

He starts to kiss GEORGE's chest. As he does, THEO appears outside the room and starts to bang on the 'door'. He's very drunk.

THEO: Hey! Hey!

JAMIE: Jesus!

THEO: Are you in there? Let me in!

GEORGE: Who's that?

JAMIE: Never mind. Look–

THEO: Hey! I know you're in there! Open the door!

JAMIE: Get in the closet!

GEORGE: What?

JAMIE: I said get in the closet!

GEORGE: Look here–

JAMIE: (*Hisses.*) Now!

GEORGE mimes getting in the closet as THEO continues to bang on the door. When GEORGE is safely hidden, JAMIE opens the door.

THEO: I heard voices.

JAMIE: Next door.

THEO: What?

JAMIE: They's people next door. That's the voices.

THEO: (*Yells.*) How stupid do you think I am?

JAMIE: I'd need a minute to think about that one, dearie.

THEO sways stupidly in the middle of the room, trying to make something out through the fog of his drunkenness. He points a finger at JAMIE.

THEO: You... you...

JAMIE: What's it to you? What's it to you what I do and don't do here? I don't recall we got any special arrangement. You come here. I give you what you want, and you give me what I need. That's all. (*Taking a paper packet from his pocket.*) Well, guess what? Tonight it's free. You don't gotta do nothing. (*He tosses it on the bed.*) Take it and go.

THEO: (*Sullenly.*) I don't want that.

JAMIE: No? What do you want? (*THEO doesn't answer; he sits on the bed.*) You're drunk. (*THEO still says nothing.*) What a pretty picture! Look at you! (*Silence.*) Honey, you're taking up space I'd reserved for other purposes.

THEO: (*Looking up.*) No!

JAMIE: (*Mockingly.*) No? No?

THEO: (*Shakes his head.*) Don't do me like that. Don't do me like that.

JAMIE: (*Impatiently.*) Like what?

THEO slips forward onto his knees and pulls JAMIE towards him.

THEO: Why you gotta be mean to me?

JAMIE: (*Glancing helplessly at the closet door.*) Awwwww. Now he's sorry. Now he's on his knees. I don't got time for it, mister. Go away and come back tomorrow.

THEO pulls JAMIE down to his knees. He wraps his arms round him roughly, nuzzling him. JAMIE resists, but he is fighting his own longing. His eyes begin to close, and his fingers move through THEO's hair. With an effort of will, he remembers GEORGE in the closet. He pushes THEO away from him, staggers towards the door, and opens it.

Get out!

THEO: (*An ominous growl.*) Get out?

JAMIE: You heard me. Get out! I told you, I don't got time for it.

THEO: No!

He surges violently to his feet. He picks up JAMIE and hurls him on the bed, pinning him to it. With each phrase he administers soft sharp slaps to JAMIE's face.

I'm not getting out. I'm not coming back tomorrow. Understand? I'm staying right here. I don't want no one coming round here when I'm not here. You understand? You understand? You're mine. You don't go with nobody but me. You're my baby. I catch you with somebody else, I'll kill you. Huh? Huh? Understand?

JAMIE: OK, honey. Yeah. Yeah. I understand. Just be quiet now. Just be quiet.

He strokes THEO's hair, as THEO slumps against him, rubbing his head against JAMIE's chest like a dog.

THEO: (*Sleepily.*) You're my baby…

GEORGE steps out of the closet and makes his report.

GEORGE: Through the keyhole, I observed both suspects engage in several unnatural and perverted acts. When they were done, suspect Jamie Peacock persuaded suspect Theo Navarro to leave the room with him, and I was able to leave my hiding place and retrieve this.

He holds up the paper packet that JAMIE threw on the bed. MR VOLE enters downstage, GEORGE crosses to meet him.

MR VOLE: Good work, good work, George! Now get me the Reverend! We need the Reverend!

GEORGE: I'm meeting him tonight, sir.

MR VOLE: You're a credit to the Navy, my boy. Dismissed.

They exit separately. JAMIE and THEO leave the bed. ELLA appears, throws a different coverlet and another pillow on it, and exits. The REVEREND enters and stands next to the bed in his pajamas and robe. He speaks to someone offstage.

REVEREND: I hope those pajamas fit. You're such a husky chap. It often happens in the course of my duties that I will have a sailor or some other lonely young man to spend the night, and I try to keep fresh nightclothes for them, but sizes and builds vary, you know, from man to man. Do they fit? (*Pause. No answer. The REVEREND sits on the bed and strokes the covers absently.*) You mustn't ever be ashamed, you know, of feeling lonely. A young chap, far away from home for the first time, is subject to it. There's nothing unmanly about it, nothing at all. In my line of work, I assure you, one quickly learns that loneliness is all too common—all too common—an affliction.

GEORGE enters in pajamas and robe.

GEORGE: Well, like I said, it's just since my buddy left the Navy. We was palling around together all the time.

REVEREND: Isn't that…sad? (*He stands up and folds back the bedcovers.*) Shall we?

They take off their robes and get into bed.

Are you quite comfortable? This old bed is not as… Here. (*He puts his arms around GEORGE.*) Is this cozier? Yes, that's nicer, isn't it? There's more than one cure for loneliness, you know. (*They begin to rub up against each other.*) Oh my! You *are* a husky young man! Now, that's lovely, isn't it? Hmmm. Yes. (*After a moment more, murmurs.*) I'm all yours, you know.

GEORGE: You want to take me?

REVEREND: Hmmmmm.

GEORGE: What way?

REVEREND: (*A little embarrassed.*) Oh, well, any old way will do.

GEORGE roughly shoves the REVEREND's head under the covers. The REVEREND emerges immediately, red-faced and spluttering.

Oh, no! No! I'm afraid–there's been a misunderstanding. *I* never do–such things. I thought that *you*–

GEORGE: You're out of your mind!

REVEREND: Oh, dear. This *is* awkward. But you and I both know that when such situations arise–as arise they will– well, there's more than one way to skin a cat. If we just do (*Pulling GEORGE close to him.*) like so. Hm. Yes. And like so. Yes. That's it. That's it. Oh my… Oh my… Oh *my*!

DR CRANKY and MR VOLE appear downstage as the REVEREND and GEORGE exit, taking the REVEREND's coverlet and pillow with them.

ELLA: My only question now, Mr Vole, is why do you hesitate? Surely the Navy has enough evidence to fall upon these men with all the fury at its disposal.

MR VOLE: More than enough, doctor. More than enough. But this brings us to a delicate question.

ELLA: (*Uncomfortably.*) You refer to the Reverend Hutch.

MR VOLE: Yes. There is some question as to whether arresting these sailors now might not 'start the hare', so to speak. We are waiting, in short, for the civil authorities to move against the Reverend.

ELLA: Mr Vole, military justice is swift and unsparing. It is not trammeled by niceties of due process and civil rights. The law of the state, alas, has not so free a hand. It necessarily moves more slowly.

MR VOLE: But I have evidence! He's committed acts of indecency against four of my men and–

ELLA: (*Sharply.*) The evidence required to arrest a sailor, Mr Vole, is not the same as that required to arrest a man of the cloth. Not at least in Newport, Rhode Island, I'm happy to say.

MR VOLE: Then, sir, we're at an impasse. The Navy–and, I need hardly add, at the highest levels–deems it essential that the Reverend Hutch be arrested, and we can hardly move against these sailors until the civil arm is ready to move with us.

ELLA: Mr Vole, you are not, I think, a married man.

MR VOLE: No, sir, I am not.

ELLA: Well, sir, as the father of daughters–daughters who have welcomed sailors into their homes, who have sat side by side with them at the pianoforte at afternoon entertainments–it is the safety of these innocent girls that I am concerned with. I urge the Navy to act against these men with all the merciless speed of which it is capable.

MR VOLE: Dr Cranky, I am not, as you point out, a married man. But I am an officer in good standing in the United States Navy and, as surely as you have the welfare of your daughters at heart, so have I the moral health of these young men to consider. Your Reverend Hutch is corrupting my men. He must be stopped.

ELLA: And he will be! *In time*! (*Pause.*) Mr Vole, arrest these men, lock them up and destroy the key, and I will see to the Reverend Hutch. He will not elude us. I promise you that.

They go. THEO and JAMIE appear in the room at the Y.

THEO: What's the matter with you?

JAMIE: What's the matter with me? You come around here drunk, tearing up the place, then I don't see you for a week.

THEO: I had some thinking to do.

JAMIE: *Thinking? You?*

THEO: Yeah, I was thinking.

JAMIE: Drinking, you mean.

THEO: I ain't drunk.

JAMIE: Oooh, Miss Carrie Nation!

THEO: Look, I come to give you something, but I ain't gonna give it to you, if you're gonna be mean.

JAMIE: *You're* gonna give *me* something. That's a switch. (*Hesitates; curious in spite of himself.*) Well, what is it?

THEO: Uh-uh. Not if you won't be nice.

JAMIE: What's nice?

THEO: (*Kisses him; JAMIE is startled.*) *That*'s nice. There now. I just give you something I never give you before. And I got something else, too. (*He takes something from his pocket. It's a ring.*) See here. I got it engraved. 'Jamie and Theo.'

JAMIE: (*Hesitates; then abruptly.*) Take it back.

THEO: Take it *back*?

JAMIE: Take it back where it come from. You got no call for that.

THEO: (*Angrily.*) Listen, you! I hawked my gold watch to get you this!

JAMIE: Well, you can get it back now. I don't need that shit. You just trade it back in for–

THEO grabs JAMIE by the back of his head and brings their lips together, kissing him roughly. JAMIE resists, then slowly yields. THEO takes hold of his hand and, without ceasing to kiss him, slips the ring on his finger. They pull apart.

THEO: All right, then?

JAMIE: I reckon so.

They stand shyly together a moment, then move towards the bed. THEO is laying JAMIE down on the bed when a banging is heard. GEORGE, playing a MILITARY POLICEMAN, has appeared outside the room.

GEORGE: Open up! Military police!

JAMIE: Jesus Christ!

Without waiting, the MP breaks down the door.

GEORGE: Pharmacist's Mate James Peacock and Seaman First Class Theobald Navarro, you are both under arrest for committing acts of gross indecency, trafficking in and use of drugs, sodomy, lewd acts, corruption of–

THEO: (*Furiously.*) Motherfucker!

He hurls himself at the MP, knocking him down; but immediately the two other Decoys, also playing MPs, rush in and subdue him. As JAMIE and THEO are led out, a judge's bench is quickly slapped together, perhaps by placing a chair on top of a table. The PROFESSOR enters, putting on the jacket of a naval officer.

PROFESSOR: It is now my melancholy duty to perform the role of military justice…such as it is…as the presiding officer of the Naval court of inquiry into this most unfortunate affair.

He climbs the bench and bangs the gavel. JAMIE, THEO, PETEY, and CHUCK enter and stand handcuffed on his right. The Decoys are on the left, VERN and MICK standing, GEORGE seated in the witness stand.

And then what happened, Mr Doerner?

GEORGE: Well, sir, the accused wanted me to brown him.

PROFESSOR: Please clarify your term, sailor, 'brown him'.

GEORGE: I mean, to push my prick in his ass, sir.

PROFESSOR: I see. Continue.

GEORGE: But we had no room to go to, so we went up on the Cliff Walk and I stood against a fence while he went down on me.

PROFESSOR: Again, the court is unfamiliar with your term.

GEORGE: He sucked my cock.

PROFESSOR: I see.

GEORGE: I mean, he held my penis in his mouth until there was emission.

PROFESSOR: Abundantly clear. I think that will be sufficient, Mr Doerner.

GEORGE descends from the witness stand and stands with the other Decoys.

In light of the evidence presented here today, this court of inquiry is prepared to make a recommendation. We recommend that each of the accused be tried by court-martial for the various crimes reviewed here, including sodomy, oral coition, trafficking in drugs, and corruption of general morals. We turn the prisoners over to the post brig to await trial.

We should not like to conclude this inquiry, however, without commending the zeal with which these young sailors have conducted their investigation. The Navy owes you a debt of gratitude, gentlemen, which it would be difficult to repay.

This court of inquiry is now adjourned.

He bangs the gavel as the Decoys and Fairies exit separately taking the judge's bench with them. DR CRANKY and MR VOLE enter separately and meet downstage center.

ELLA: May I congratulate you, Mr Vole, on the success of your prosecutions?

MR VOLE: You flatter me, Dr Cranky. It was all in the line of duty. Might I inquire about the progress of...the other matter?

ELLA: It is being taken care of even as we speak. The success of your own prosecution has sped it along.

MR VOLE: I'm very glad to hear it, Dr Cranky. Good day.

ELLA: Good day, Mr Vole.

They exit separately. In the YMCA room, the PROFESSOR *sits at his desk writing. The* REVEREND *appears outside and taps cautiously at the door. The* PROFESSOR *rises and opens it.*

PROFESSOR: Reverend Hutch! This is a pleasant surprise! I don't believe I've ever had the honor of a visit from you.

REVEREND: (*Nervously.*) No, no. Long overdue. Tending to others of my flock. (*Seeing the open notebook on the desk.*) But I interrupt your work, Professor.

PROFESSOR: Not at all. I'm afraid I was accomplishing nothing. Perhaps your visit will inspire.

REVEREND: (*A little joke.*) Yes, well, I'm in the business of inspiration, you know.

They both laugh, then fall into an awkward silence.

PROFESSOR: Could I offer you any–? I'm afraid I don't–

REVEREND: Oh, no, no, not at all.

Pause.

PROFESSOR: I hope it won't be impolite of me to remark that you seem troubled today, Reverend.

REVEREND: Yes, yes, perhaps… (*Pause.*) If I might– (*Indicates the bed and sits.*)

PROFESSOR: Of course, of course.

He sits in the chair and another silence ensues.

REVEREND: Professor, you're a young chap of understanding. You have studied the world.

PROFESSOR: I hope I have only just begun.

REVEREND: But still, I think you will understand when I tell you that my situation, just at the moment, is slightly irregular.

PROFESSOR: In what way, Reverend?

REVEREND: It seems–

They are interrupted by the appearance of GEORGE, *playing a* POLICEMAN.

GEORGE: (*Banging on the door.*) Open up! Police!

REVEREND: Oh, dear, oh, dear. Professor, if I might– (*He indicates the closet.*)

PROFESSOR: Be my guest, Reverend.

REVEREND: And you won't mention–

PROFESSOR: No, no, of course not.

The REVEREND *mimes hiding in the closet, and as the* POLICEMAN *knocks again, the* PROFESSOR *lets him in.*

GEORGE: I'm looking for the Reverend Edward Hutch.

PROFESSOR: I'm afraid I don't have the honor to be that gentleman.

GEORGE: No, no. But we thought he came in this direction.

PROFESSOR: You perhaps require his assistance for–

GEORGE: I've come to arrest him!

PROFESSOR: On what charge?

GEORGE: Indecency!

PROFESSOR: Oh dear. Well, if only I could be of service to you, but as it happens–

The POLICEMAN *walks over to the* PROFESSOR's *desk and begins to flip through his notebook.*

I really prefer, officer, that people don't–

A sneeze comes from the closet.

GEORGE: Bless you.

PROFESSOR: Thank you.

As the POLICEMAN *turns to him, the* PROFESSOR *wipes self-consciously at his nose.*

GEORGE: Well, if you see him–

PROFESSOR: I will direct him immediately to your attention.

The POLICEMAN leaves, and after a moment, the REVEREND emerges from the closet.

REVEREND: I owe you a debt of gratitude.

PROFESSOR: Please don't mention it. We owe it to our fellow travelers…

REVEREND: (*Sitting disconsolately on the bed.*) Yes, yes. I hope that I have not compromised you in any–

PROFESSOR: Not at all.

REVEREND: It's just, you see, that my situation is really quite irregular. Certain accusations–accusations, I need hardly add, which I refute utterly–have been flung at my head and the hounds of the law have been loosed at my heels.

PROFESSOR: But surely an innocent man has no need to fear from–

REVEREND: If only that were true, Professor, if only. But I am older than you and, at the risk of tarnishing your young ideals, I must say that the world is an unjust place.

PROFESSOR: It is indeed, Reverend.

Silence.

REVEREND: Can you advise me in any way?

PROFESSOR: Without understanding your situation, alas, I cannot. You are, however, welcome to remain here as long as necessary.

REVEREND: (*Gazing longingly at the closet.*) But a man can't hide away forever.

PROFESSOR: The question of what a man is capable of is one I have not yet plumbed, Reverend.

Pause.

REVEREND: You advise me then to give myself up?

PROFESSOR: If the only alternative is to hide in my closet, then perhaps…you might give that option its due consideration.

Pause. The REVEREND sighs and stands up.

REVEREND: You're right, Professor. How refreshing it is to talk now and then with a man of understanding.

He moves sadly to the door, followed by the PROFESSOR. As he steps outside, the POLICEMAN approaches.

GEORGE: Reverend Edward Hutch? You'll have to come with me.

MR VOLE appears from the shadows.

MR VOLE: Yes, Reverend, it's the end of the trail for you.

As the POLICEMAN leads the REVEREND off, MR VOLE turns to the PROFESSOR.

I knew I could count on you, Professor. Always a treat to deal with a man of real understanding.

The PROFESSOR looks unhappily after MR VOLE as he follows the others offstage. Blackout.

Act II

A bare stage. The PROFESSOR enters.

PROFESSOR: Let us, for argument's sake, say that our first act was about Vice. In the second act we take up the theme of Justice. Justice… The Ancients defined it as 'everything in its place'. And what is our longing for Justice but a hope that everything will return to its place, that underlying the chaotic jumble of our lives is a supreme eternal Order to which our every action tends? This hope flickers within us, even in our darkest hours.

Justice, then. How often cried out for! How seldom encountered! And when encountered, in what strange, unrecognizable shapes!

Before we continue, however, no public forum is complete until we have heard from that most voluble of organs, the American press, bulwark of our most cherished freedoms.

PETEY appears as MR PUMPHREY. He wears a vividly checked suit, amply padded in the stomach, and a racing cap.

Mr Abel Pumphrey, editor of the *Providence (Rhode Island) Journal.*

PETEY: (*Waving a copy of the* Journal.) 'NEWPORT CLERIC ARRESTED ON VICE CHARGE'! (*Opens to the editorial page.*) The arrest of the Reverend Edward James Hutch by the United States Navy on charges of indecency must shock and dismay all right-thinking men. We at the *Providence Journal* can only stand in fearful silence at such a spectacle. We trust that the Navy has considered carefully before pressing such a course against a man of the cloth, particularly one of such unblemished repute. We tremble to think of the cost not only to the good father's reputation, but to the reputation indeed of the Navy, if they have acted rashly or precipitately in their pursuit of this scandalous charge.

PROFESSOR: Thank you, Mr Pumphrey.

MR PUMPHREY bows and exits.

Now, Justice.

A judge's black robe flies from the wings, and he catches it in mid-flight.

This is the part I shall endeavor to play for much of the next hour. (*He puts on the robe.*) But we will need our courtroom back. (*The judge's bench is reassembled.*) There. (*He ascends the bench and calls:*) Defendant! (*The REVEREND appears.*) And the attorneys. For the prosecution… (*THEO enters, wearing a suit, as the prosecuting attorney.*) And for the defense… (*JAMIE enters, also in a suit.*)

REVEREND: Professor, I really must object. *This* (*Pointing to JAMIE.*) is my *defense* attorney?

JAMIE: I *beg* your pardon!

PROFESSOR: (*Placatingly.*) Reverend, perhaps you missed my earlier explanation to the audience. We are terribly short on actors and, owing to some questions about the morality of the piece–

REVEREND: My story is *not* immoral!

PROFESSOR: As we have tried to explain to the applicable agencies. But we are nevertheless still sorely underfunded, and hence–

REVEREND: But *this* man–*this* man as my *defense*?

JAMIE: Oh, stow it, sister! You'll get yours. You were expecting Clarence Darrow?

PROFESSOR: Gentlemen, please. If we could begin–

He indicates the two attorneys. They bow to each other.

THEO: Mr Haney.

JAMIE: Mr Chump.

THEO: The State will call as its first witness Ezekiel Vole.

MR VOLE enters and assumes the witness stand. Everyone waits expectantly, looking at the PROFESSOR, who suddenly realizes:

PROFESSOR: (*Calls.*) Bailiff? (*No answer; he looks around helplessly.*) Oh, dear. (*He turns to MR VOLE.*) You swear to tell the truth, the whole truth, and nothing but the truth so help you God?

MR VOLE: I do.

PROFESSOR: (*To THEO.*) Proceed.

THEO: Mr Vole, you were entrusted by the Navy with a certain investigation, were you not?

MR VOLE: I was, sir.

THEO: Can you describe it to the court?

MR VOLE: I was ordered by the Navy to investigate conditions of vice around the Newport naval base.

THEO: And for what reasons was this investigation entrusted to you?

MR VOLE: Begging the court's pardon, I'm something of an expert on perverts. I got to know their habits during nine years running them down for the Connecticut State Police. I can tell nine times out of ten, by a suspect's feminine speech or peculiar walk, whether they're a degenerate of a nameless type.

THEO: And your investigation discovered several of these degenerates in Newport?

MR VOLE: A great many, I'm sorry to say.

THEO: Was the defendant among them?

MR VOLE: Several of the men on my team reported improper advances made on them by the Reverend Hutch. I have their reports here.

He hands the reports to THEO.

THEO: Your honor, I would like to enter these into evidence.

He tries to hand the reports to the PROFESSOR, *but* JAMIE *snatches them from him. He gives them only a careless glance, however, before handing them on to the* PROFESSOR *with a bored gesture.* THEO *glares at him.*

(*To* MR VOLE.) And what conclusion did you draw from these reports, Mr Vole?

MR VOLE: That the Reverend Edward James Hutch is a pervert of the worst description.

THEO: Thank you, Mr Vole. That will be all.

PROFESSOR: Mr Haney?

JAMIE: No questions, your honor.

REVEREND: No *questions*?

JAMIE: No questions.

PROFESSOR: Mr Chump, you may call your next witness.

THEO: Your honor, the State calls Vernon M Tetchill to the stand.

MR VOLE exits and VERN *enters, assuming the witness stand.*

PROFESSOR: You swear to tell the truth, the whole truth, et cetera, et cetera.

VERN: Yes.

PROFESSOR: (*To* THEO.) Proceed.

THEO: Mr Tetchill, will you describe how you came to know the defendant?

VERN: Which one?

THEO: (*Patiently.*) The Reverend Edward Hutch.

VERN: He give me a ride.

THEO: That was kind of him.

VERN: No, sir.

THEO: Why not?

VERN: He took liberties.

THEO: What sort of liberties?

VERN: He fondled my privates, sir.

THEO: And what did you do?

VERN: Nothing, sir.

THEO: And then what happened?

VERN: He took my penis out and began to play with it.

THEO: And what did you do?

VERN: Nothing, sir.

THEO: And then what happened?

VERN: I went off, sir.

THEO: You had an emission?

VERN: Yes, sir. And then he drove me home.

THEO: I see. Thank you. No further questions.

JAMIE: Mr Tetchill…

VERN: (*Looking about in confusion.*) Huh?

JAMIE: Over here, dear. Mr Tetchill, why did you first get into the car with Reverend Hutch?

VERN: We was told to find out what we could about the Reverend. To find out if he was an immoral man.

JAMIE: Who told you to do so?

VERN: Mr Vole did.

JAMIE: Mr Vole told you to go with Reverend Hutch?

VERN: Yes, sir.

JAMIE: To allow him to play with your privates?

VERN: Yes, sir.

JAMIE: Until you had an emission?

VERN: If necessary, sir.

JAMIE: Thank you, Mr Tetchill. No further questions.

THEO: The state calls Michael McGeary to the stand.

VERN leaves the stand and MICK enters and takes his place. THEO looks expectantly at the PROFESSOR who looks puzzled, then remembers and turns to MICK.

PROFESSOR: The truth?

MICK: Yes, sir.

THEO: Mr McGeary, would you describe what occurred between you and Reverend Hutch on the night of April 20, 1919?

MICK: Reverend Hutch invited me to spend the night at his home. When we arrived, he made up the bed and we got in it. He offered to kiss me and fondled me until I had achieved a state of excitement—I mean—that is—*rigidity*. He then rubbed up against me until we both discharged.

THEO: And then?

MICK: We slept and I left as soon as possible the following morning.

THEO: Thank you. Mr Haney?

JAMIE: Mr McGeary, were you instructed as well by Mr Vole to go out with Reverend Hutch?

MICK: Yes, sir.

JAMIE: You had been told he was an immoral man?

MICK: Yes, sir.

JAMIE: And believing him to be an immoral man, you went to his home?

MICK: Those were my instructions, sir.

JAMIE: From Mr Vole?

MICK: Yes, sir.

JAMIE: And in his room, the events you describe took place?

MICK: That's right.

JAMIE: Was this the first time you had done such a thing?

MICK: Sir?

JAMIE: Was this the first time you had gone up to a man's room and let him play with your privates?

THEO: Objection. This is irrelevant to the proceeding at hand.

JAMIE: Your honor, serious accusations have been made against my client. I think we are obliged to determine the character and general trustworthiness of those making the accusations.

PROFESSOR: The witness will answer the question.

MICK: Our instructions from Mr Vole were to find out about the men of low character in Newport.

JAMIE: And, therefore, you did this with several men?

MICK: A few sir.

JAMIE: Allowed them to play with your instrument until emission?

MICK: Yes, sir.

JAMIE: Did you ever allow your instrument to be sucked?

MICK: On occasion, sir.

JAMIE: And did you, in turn, suck?

MICK: Never, sir.

JAMIE: Did you perform sodomy?

MICK: Sodomy, sir?

JAMIE: Did you enter any man in his rectum?

MICK: Only once as I recall, sir.

JAMIE: Only once as you recall. Was it…in the line of duty?

MICK: Yes, sir.

JAMIE: May I ask, Mr McGeary, if you *enjoyed* your work?

THEO: Objection!

PROFESSOR: Sustained.

JAMIE: No further questions, your honor.

The principals depart abruptly from the stage, and the PROFESSOR descends from the bench. He drapes the judicial robe over his arm and addresses the audience.

PROFESSOR: Justice. Or our own poor approximation thereof. We are adjourning briefly to visit one of the other halls of Justice. You may have been wondering what happened with the young men who fell into her net in the previous act. Rest assured, Justice has not been idle. After several months of incarceration, the men were brought before courts-martial, duly tried, and sentenced. The list of charges, verdicts, and punishments would be long, since many more men were involved than we can show here with our meager resources. But we can show you two now, sentenced to twenty years in the Navy brig for indecency, sodomy, and traffic in cocaine.

He leaves the stage. A shadowy darkness falls over it with a pattern of jail bars projected against the floor. JAMIE and THEO enter from opposite sides, dressed in prison uniforms.

JAMIE: Theo?

THEO: Jamie?

They approach each other.

JAMIE: How ya doing?

THEO: OK. (*Beat.*) You?

JAMIE: All right. (*He touches THEO's arm.*) Theo… I can't do it. It's too long. I won't last. Not here. I can't do it. (*Silence. THEO says nothing.*) Theo? Are you listening? Say something. I can't do it, Theo.

THEO: I can.

JAMIE: What?

THEO: I can. I can wait. Twenty years. For you.

JAMIE: Theo…

THEO: (*Shaking off JAMIE's hand.*) Don't you wanna know how?

JAMIE: How?

THEO: (*He puts his hand on JAMIE's cheek and strokes it roughly.*) Cause all that time I'll be thinking about what I'm gonna do to you when I get out. I'll be planning it. I haven't decided how yet, but I got twenty years to think about it, and I'll do it. I'm gonna kill you. So you wait, too. You wait for me. I wanna see the look on your face when I do it. I wanna see you die. Then I don't care what happens. They can haul me back here, they can string me up. I'll swing happy, knowing you're dead and knowing I done it.

JAMIE: (*Grabbing THEO's arm.*) Theo!

THEO raises his hand to strike JAMIE, but just then GEORGE enters as a PRISON GUARD.

GEORGE: You there! Break it up!

He brings his club down on JAMIE's arm, forcing JAMIE to let go of THEO. The GUARD drags THEO off as JAMIE nurses his arm.

THEO: (*Turning to JAMIE.*) Look what you done to me!

The lights go out. A spot comes up downstage on PETEY as MR PUMPHREY.

PETEY: We at the *Providence Journal* must confess ourselves something feeble of understanding. It seems to us—though we know this cannot be—that sailors in the United States Navy have been—and here we beg our female subscribers to read no further—have been instructed in the details of a nameless vice in order to entrap reputable members of the Newport clergy. We know this cannot be so, and it is only the insufficiency of our own weak wits that makes it appear so.

MR PUMPHREY exits. ELLA, as DR CRANKY, appears on one side of the stage. As he crosses the stage, he stops suddenly in dismay. He looks for an avenue of escape. Too late. VERN appears on the other side of the stage in a bowler hat and suit. He speaks loudly but slowly, as if he is a man of strong opinions but limited brainpower.

VERN: CRANKY!

ELLA: Oh, good evening, Senator Bullrose!

VERN: WHAT THE HELL IS GOING ON HERE, CRANKY? I'VE GOT CONSTITUENTS SENDING ME LETTERS! THEY'RE CALLING MY WIFE! EVERYONE WANTS TO KNOW WHAT THE HELL IS GOING ON!

ELLA: The situation is indeed unfortunate…

VERN: SINCE WHEN DOES THE U.S. NAVY TRAIN THE BOYS TO BUGGER EACH OTHER??!!

ELLA: I assure you I had no idea that anything of the sort was…

VERN: WASN'T THAT WAY WHEN I WAS IN THE NAVY. WE LEARNED ROPE-TYING. SEMAPHORES. PLAYED THE HORNPIPE. NOT SODOMY!! WHO IS THIS GUY ANYWAY?

ELLA: Mr Vole is a Chief Machinist's Mate.

VERN: MACHINIST'S MATE?? THEY DON'T PUT A MACHINIST'S MATE IN CHARGE OF INVESTIGATIONS. WHO PUT HIM UP TO THIS?

ELLA: Mr Vole assured me that his orders came from the very highest sources. Indeed from Secretary Roosevelt himself.

A crafty light comes into the SENATOR's eye.

VERN: Roosevelt, eh?

ELLA: He is, as you know… (*A delicate cough.*) a Democrat.

VERN: (*Grinning broadly.*) He is indeed. Dr Cranky, let's say you and I pay a visit on Mr Pumphrey at the *Journal.*

As they walk off arm in arm, the courtroom re-appears with the principals.

THEO: The State calls George Doerner to the stand.

GEORGE takes the witness stand.

Mr Doerner, you are acquainted with the defendant?

GEORGE: I've had the misfortune to run into him once or twice.

THEO: Under what circumstances?

GEORGE: The Reverend Hutch invited me out on several occasions and once had me spend the night at his house.

THEO: And what transpired?

GEORGE: Mr Hutch began to fondle me.

THEO: What do you mean by 'fondle'?

GEORGE: He put his hand on my knee in a very suggestive manner and told me what a fine young man I was.

THEO: What happened then?

GEORGE: We got into bed together. And then he pressed up against me and told me that's what two men do when they think well of each other.

THEO: What did he do then?

GEORGE: He began to play with my tool–

THEO: Your–?

GEORGE: My penis, sir. And told me how large it was. Is.

THEO: Did he offer any further indecencies?

GEORGE: He rubbed his penis up against me, sir, until we both came–uh–discharged.

THEO: Thank you, Mr Doerner. No further questions.

JAMIE: Mr Doerner, when the defendant offered these alleged indecencies to you, did you strike him?

GEORGE: No, sir.

JAMIE: Did you resist?

GEORGE: No, sir.

JAMIE: Did you protest?

GEORGE: No, sir.

JAMIE: Did you get up and leave the Reverend's home?

GEORGE: No, sir.

JAMIE: Why not?

GEORGE: My instructions were to play along as much as possible.

JAMIE: Your instructions? From whom?

GEORGE: Mr Vole.

JAMIE: Ah, yes. Mr Vole. And he instructed you to go to Reverend Hutch's home and allow him to play with your instrument?

GEORGE: I was to gather evidence against Mr Hutch. Those were my orders.

JAMIE: Your orders were to allow him to fondle your penis until emission?

GEORGE: It wasn't so particular, sir. We was to use our own judgment. We was to go as far as was necessary.

JAMIE: And you did do this with other men as well?

THEO: Objection!

JAMIE: Oh, *please*!

PROFESSOR: Overruled.

GEORGE: In the process of gathering evidence, yes, sir.

JAMIE: You were ordered to do so?

GEORGE: I was ordered to gather evidence.

JAMIE: And you understood by this that you were to let your instrument be fondled?

GEORGE: If necessary, sir.

JAMIE: To let it be sucked?

GEORGE: To do whatever was required.

JAMIE: Until emission?

GEORGE: The emission was involuntary, sir.

JAMIE: I see. Mr Doerner, how did you like your work?

THEO: Objection!

PROFESSOR: I'll allow it this time.

GEORGE: I didn't particularly.

JAMIE: Were you forced to perform it?

GEORGE: I– We volunteered.

JAMIE: Did you ever ask to get out of it?

GEORGE: No, sir.

JAMIE: Why not?

GEORGE: I liked the principle too much.

JAMIE: The principle?

GEORGE: These fellows, they make me sick. Prancing about. Making themselves up like women. It's disgusting. They're sick. And they want to make everyone else the way they are. I was happy to help rid the service of them.

JAMIE: I see. The Navy, I'm sure, owes you its highest commendation for your…efforts. Where are you from, Mr Doerner?

GEORGE: Michigan.

JAMIE: Have you a mother living, Mr Doerner?

GEORGE: Yes, sir.

JAMIE: What would she have thought of your...duties?

THEO: Objection!

PROFESSOR: Sustained.

JAMIE: No further questions.

MR PUMPHREY takes up a spot downstage.

PETEY: We must ask—we *do* ask—where the final responsibility for this lies. Boys, sent by their mothers to serve in the Navy's glorious and honorable tradition, have instead been instructed in the particulars of a nameless vice, have been encouraged to practice this vice in the interests of an 'investigation'. At whose hands has the lustrous reputation of the United States Navy been so besmirched? We at the *Providence Journal* have reason to believe that the trail of blame leads very high indeed, even to the office of the Secretary of the Navy himself, Mr Franklin Roosevelt. Mr Roosevelt, what have you to say to the mothers of America?

MR PUMPHREY exits. A table appears with ROOSEVELT, played by CHUCK, sitting behind it. His jaws are clamped around a cigarette holder, the first sign that CHUCK's Roosevelt impersonation will be painfully over-the-top. MICK plays his AIDE.

CHUCK: (*Waving a copy of the* Providence Journal.) I want a letter to Mr Abel Pumphrey of the *Providence Journal* informing him that any further attempt to drag my name into the sordid affair at Newport will result in a libel suit. Or better yet, advise Mr Pumphrey that his continued effort to dishonor the reputation of the United States Navy will be viewed in the light of the applicable treason laws.

MICK: Perhaps a little heavy-handed, Mr Roosevelt?

CHUCK: *Heavy-handed*? Do you know what the Republicans are saying in the Senate? They're out for my blood. What was this Vole chap thinking anyway? A few sailors, yes. No one objects to arresting some sailors. Cleans the place up a bit. But you don't send the Navy in after an Episcopal priest!

MICK: I only meant to suggest, sir, that perhaps a softer *tone* is required. *This* arrived today. (*He hands ROOSEVELT a letter.*)

CHUCK: What is it?

MICK: It's a petition, sir. From the clergy of Newport. It asks you to take a personal interest in this Newport business—an interest, that is to say, *for* Reverend Hutch and *against* the Vole investigation.

CHUCK: (*Raising his eyebrows.*) Strongly worded.

MICK: For clergymen, yes, I would say so, sir.

CHUCK: This arrived today?

MICK: Yes.

CHUCK: (*Suspiciously.*) How?

MICK: It was personally delivered by Bishop Henry Pierce Woollett of the Episcopal Church in Rhode Island. He attends your leisure in the outer office.

CHUCK: Oh God.

MICK: He sends his compliments to your mother with whom he enjoys a passing acquaintance.

CHUCK: (*Head in hands.*) Oh God. Send him in.

The courtroom reappears.

PROFESSOR: Mr Haney, is the defense ready to present its case?

JAMIE: Yes, your honor. We call the Reverend Edward James Hutch to the stand.

The REVEREND assumes the witness stand.

You are the Reverend Edward James Hutch.

REVEREND: I am.

JAMIE: You have worked a great deal with young men, Reverend?

REVEREND: Yes, it is a particular talent of mine, I suppose. I directed young people's religious programs in New York and was housemaster at a religious residence for boys in Pennsylvania. And, of course, my work for the last two years as a Navy chaplain has been largely with young men.

JAMIE: In all modesty, Reverend, what was your reputation at these places?

REVEREND: In modesty, sir, I would say my reputation was considered to be entirely without blemish.

JAMIE: Was there ever a word of blame?

REVEREND: No, sir.

JAMIE: Of censure?

REVEREND: No, sir.

JAMIE: Of scandal?

REVEREND: No, sir. I believe my work and my morals were universally approved.

JAMIE: In the course of your ministry, Reverend, is it your custom to invite young men to spend the night at your home?

REVEREND: It is not only *my* custom, sir, but the custom of many of my colleagues.

JAMIE: Under what circumstances would you do so?

REVEREND: If a young man, away from familiar surroundings, seemed particularly troubled or lonely or in need of spiritual guidance, I would on occasion offer him the comforts of a warm home and my own religious counsel.

JAMIE: Now I must ask you some painful questions, Reverend. You are familiar with George Doerner?

REVEREND: Yes, sir.

JAMIE: And you have heard his testimony against you in this court?

REVEREND: Yes, sir.

JAMIE: You recall the night in question?

REVEREND: I do.

JAMIE: Can you tell us what occurred?

REVEREND: I had invited Mr Doerner to spend the night at my home because he said he was lonely. As we got ready for bed, I set up a cot for him in the adjoining room. When I got into bed, however, he appeared in my room and got in bed beside me and asked if we could not have a good time. He put his arms about me and rubbed his…parts against me. I noticed that he had an erection. I remonstrated with him sharply, but he persisted. At last I forced him from the bed and bolted the door between our rooms. I need hardly say how terribly distressed I was. I had no idea what to do. In the event, I waited till morning, then drove him immediately back to town. I had nothing further to do with him.

JAMIE: What of the events described by Michael McGeary?

REVEREND: They never happened.

JAMIE: The story is false?

REVEREND: Absolutely false. On the night in question I attended a concert with Miss Ophelia T Abbott, a spinster of Forster Street. She will attest to this.

JAMIE: And what of Vernon Tetchill's testimony?

REVEREND: Mr Tetchill came to me for spiritual guidance. I took him for a ride in my automobile. In the course of my counsel I placed my hand on his knee. He seemed to misconstrue this gesture for he moved my hand immediately to his privates. I drew it sharply away and remonstrated with him severely. I told him such things are wrong for a young man, or indeed for anybody. That a chap with such a tendency must learn to overcome it and that he should cut it out altogether and at once. 'You want to be a good *clean* chap!' I said.

JAMIE: Reverend Hutch, have you ever committed improper acts with any young man in your spiritual care?

REVEREND: Never, sir. Nor with any young man at all.

JAMIE: Thank you, Reverend. You have been very patient. No further questions.

THEO: Reverend Hutch, three young men have testified in this courtroom that you committed immoral acts against their persons.

REVEREND: I have heard their testimony, sir.

THEO: Yet you absolutely deny that any of this transpired?

REVEREND: Absolutely, sir.

THEO: Why do you suppose, Reverend, that these men would make such stories up?

REVEREND: It is always perilous to speculate on the motives of others, Mr Chump, but I noticed that each young man admitted that he'd been ordered to entrap me by his superiors in the Navy. Sometimes young men, particularly impressionable young men who are far away from home for the first time, are overzealous in the commission of their duties.

THEO: I refer you to the incident described by Vernon Tetchill. You say you put your hand on his knee.

REVEREND: Yes, sir.

THEO: What business, Reverend, had your hand to be there?

REVEREND: It was a gesture of comfort.

THEO: Comfort?

REVEREND: Yes, sir.

THEO: Is it seemly, Reverend, for a man of God, for whatever reason, to put his hand on a young man's knee?

REVEREND: (*Sharply.*) My hand was in no place, sir, of which God or my superiors would not approve.

THEO: Reverend, what if I told you that your reputation, far from being universally esteemed, has fallen repeatedly under the shadow of such stories as we have heard already several times in this court?

JAMIE: Your honor! Mr Chump, having failed to make his case against my client, now seeks to convict him by hearsay and vague inference.

PROFESSOR: Please be more to the point, Mr Chump.

THEO: Reverend, are you acquainted with the sailors who were arrested for indecency this winter?

REVEREND: With some of them, of course.

THEO: Did you realize the damage done to your reputation when your name was connected with men who were arrested and tried on charges of immorality?

JAMIE: Objection!

PROFESSOR: Overruled.

REVEREND: I was unaware that my reputation was under suspicion. I might add, sir, that the example of our Lord instructs us to attend to those most in need of guidance, not those who will further enhance our reputations.

The YMCA room appears. The PROFESSOR sits at his desk. The REVEREND appears and knocks timidly. The PROFESSOR rises and opens the door.

PROFESSOR: Reverend Hutch! Once again I am honored by your visit!

REVEREND: Oh, yes, quite… That is to say… Privilege all mine…

PROFESSOR: (*After studying the REVEREND with concern a moment.*) It's quite illegal, of course, and I blush to disclose it, but some sailors made me a gift of some rather good moonshine…

REVEREND: Oh, you're a good chap, Professor!

PROFESSOR: (*Embarrassed.*) Nothing at all, Reverend. (*He pours them each a tooth-glass of whiskey.*) To your health!

REVEREND: And yours!

They drink in silence a moment.

PROFESSOR: How does the trial go, Reverend Hutch?

REVEREND: Oh, very well. Or not so well. Or—it weighs on me, you know. It's all so…difficult.

PROFESSOR: Yes, I would imagine…

REVEREND: (*Working up a little indignation.*) These scurrilous charges!

PROFESSOR: Oh, yes, quite, quite.

Pause.

REVEREND: Professor, may I ask your opinion of something?

PROFESSOR: Of course.

REVEREND: Professor, if a man of God, devoted, you understand, to the work of God, called to His service by the strongest of emotions…

PROFESSOR: We are speaking hypothetically?

REVEREND: Hypothetically, yes. If this man whose life is devoted to God, were to go into a court of law and, taking an oath in the *name* of God—

PROFESSOR: (*Quickly.*) Yes, yes, I see your point.

REVEREND: —if he were then to say things that weren't, in the strictest sense, quite exactly true… (*He pauses.*)

PROFESSOR: (*Gently.*) Yes, Reverend?

REVEREND: I mean to say, what would become of such a man?

PROFESSOR: Become of him…?

REVEREND: I mean, would he still *be* a man? Would he still… exist?

PROFESSOR: (*Considers.*) Exist? Certainly…in some sense.

REVEREND: But not in the *same* sense? He would be in some way…forever…diminished?

PROFESSOR: (*Pause.*) I really cannot say, Reverend.

REVEREND: (*Sadly.*) No more can I, Professor. There are certain points in life beyond which a chap cannot see…cannot… imagine. I have reached, I believe, such a point.

PROFESSOR: I'm sorry to hear it, Reverend.

REVEREND: Well, nothing to do but close one's eyes and cross over.

PROFESSOR: (*Dubiously.*) It's a *kind* of courage, I suppose.

After a pause, the REVEREND abruptly rises.

REVEREND: Yes, yes. I really mustn't intrude–upon your patience–a moment longer.

PROFESSOR: Not at all.

REVEREND: But I must, really, be going. Remember me in your prayers, Professor.

PROFESSOR: And me in yours.

REVEREND: (*Doubtfully.*) Oh, *my* prayers–well, yes, yes, if you insist. Good day, Professor.

PROFESSOR: Good day, Reverend Hutch.

The REVEREND exits. The PROFESSOR steps out of the YMCA room. MICK hands him a basket covered with a cloth. To the audience:

I have one more visit to relate–

MR PUMPHREY steps out on stage, holding a newspaper.

If you please, Mr Pumphrey, perhaps a little later.

MR PUMPHREY exits. The stage becomes shadowy and the silhouette of prison bars appears upstage left. JAMIE enters and sets two wooden chairs there. GEORGE enters downstage right as a PRISON GUARD and takes the PROFESSOR to JAMIE's cell. He mimes opening a cell door. In another cell across the stage, THEO sits, brooding.

GEORGE: Twenty minutes.

PROFESSOR: Thank you.

The GUARD exits.

JAMIE: Professor?

PROFESSOR: Jamie! How are you?

JAMIE: Well, Professor, I guess I'm just all right. Ain't you a doll to come visit me in my dreary little cell?

PROFESSOR: I thought you might want news of the outer world.

JAMIE: The outer world and I won't have much to do with each other for a while. Did ya hear, Professor? Twenty years.

PROFESSOR: Yes, yes, I heard. I was…most distressed.

JAMIE: Well, it's sweet of you to say so. Now, am I a greedy girl, or is there something in that basket for me?

PROFESSOR: Its entire contents, in fact—though, what one brings to a friend in prison…

JAMIE: Your sunshiny face is all a boy could require.

PROFESSOR: What I mean to say is, the question puzzled me a great deal, so I brought— (*He pulls a dish from the basket.*)

JAMIE: What? An Indian pudding!

PROFESSOR: Made by a pair of old maid sisters who have a bake shop in Croydon Lane. Their story is quite interesting. The daughters of Chinese missionaries— missionaries, I mean, to China—they were once imprisoned by—oh, dear—oh, well… And they made this lovely fruitcake, too. Really, they're quite geniuses in their simple art.

61

JAMIE: I'm floored, Professor. Give that here. (*He goes through the basket.*) Chocolate! Bay rum! Oh, Professor honey, I'd given up on ever smelling pretty again! It's too much. I can't look at it. It's too…too…much… (*He has faded off.*)

PROFESSOR: Jamie?

JAMIE: Hm? Well, I won't look at it all now. I don't want to waste your precious visit gazing at my toys. Let's sit down and have a nice chat, shall we?

They sit down.

You always been so nice to us boys. Why is that? For a while there, I thought you was one of us. But you're not, are you? Leastways, no one ever heard a thing about you. Not even a tickle in the toilet. What about it, Professor? Ain't you ever been a little bad that way?

PROFESSOR: (*Coughs in embarrassment.*) A man of the world should, I believe, be ready to explore the world in all its—aspects, but I have always felt—personally—that for the artist—such explorations are best made—at a safe distance.

JAMIE: (*Softly.*) But it's a lonely little distance, ain't it, Professor? Oh, Professor, maybe I miss that most of all. You get used to things here. My life outside wasn't such joy all the time anyway. But, oh, I miss that human touch. (*He puts his hand on the PROFESSOR's knee.*) Sometimes you can bribe a guard. Sometimes you can sneak a quick one in the laundry room. But it ain't the same. Professor, what I wouldn't give right now for one soft human touch in a loving sort of way…

He is stroking the PROFESSOR's thigh. The PROFESSOR sits very still.

You must feel it, too, Professor. Don't you? Everybody does. It can't be all up in your head, Professor. Some of it's gotta be down here.

The PROFESSOR stands up abruptly.

PROFESSOR: No!… I'm sorry…it's not…possible…

JAMIE: Can't live without love, Professor.

THEO stands up and restlessly paces his cell.

PROFESSOR: (*Turning away.*) Love…is a condition of the spirit, not…an act of the body. Yes, ideally, the corporal touch can deepen the mysterious union of souls that we call love, but in some cases—that touch—debases love—turns it into something altogether different. Between two men, love—*that* love—physical love—is, I believe, never possible. Not now. Not in our times. Perhaps for the ancients, in their wisdom, yes, but now—no—not what we, in the truest, purest sense, call love.

JAMIE: Love is a feel in the dark, Professor.

PROFESSOR: (*Turning back; smiles sadly.*) I believe our time is nearly up. Shall I visit you again?

JAMIE: Suit yourself, Professor. You got twenty years to decide.

The GUARD is approaching the cell.

PROFESSOR: Well, I shall, then.

JAMIE: I'll be here.

GEORGE: Time's up. (*He opens the door.*)

JAMIE: See ya later, Professor. Thanks for the fruitcake.

As the PROFESSOR leaves, JAMIE and THEO take up positions on the opposite sides of the stage, gazing at each other. GEORGE appears behind THEO and PETEY behind JAMIE. They help them into their lawyers' coats, like seconds at a boxing match. JAMIE and THEO continue to gaze at each other, breaking only when the courtroom and its principals appear around them.

PROFESSOR: You may continue, Mr Haney.

JAMIE: The defense calls his Excellency Bishop Henry Pierce Woollett to the stand.

CHUCK enters dressed in transparent old man guise and clerical garb. He makes an exaggeratedly feeble and palsied attempt to cross to the witness stand. After a bit of this, the PROFESSOR *looks at his watch.*

PROFESSOR: If his Excellency could hurry it up a bit.

CHUCK picks up the pace and gains the witness stand.

JAMIE: Bishop Woollett–

CHUCK: (*Cupping his ear.*) Eh?

JAMIE: (*Louder.*) Bishop Woollett, you are acquainted with the defendant?

CHUCK: *Who?*

JAMIE: (*Louder still.*) The *defendant.* Reverend Edward James Hutch.

CHUCK: Yes, sir.

JAMIE: For how long?

CHUCK: Since he first began his ministry.

JAMIE: Would you say he enjoyed a good reputation in the Church?

CHUCK: Hm?

JAMIE: (*Louder, with an annoyed look at the* PROFESSOR.) Was he a man of good repute?

CHUCK: Very good repute. Very good indeed.

JAMIE: Can you describe his reputation?

CHUCK: I can.

Pause.

JAMIE: (*Sharply.*) *Will* you–describe it?

CHUCK: Ah, yes, of course. (*CHUCK wrings every possibility for double entendre from his speech. As he does, catcalls and whoops are heard from the wings.*) He is looked upon as an earnest Christian who is much interested in *young men* and *boys*, with a general knowledge of how to *approach* young men, securing the strongest possible *hold* upon them. Many a young man has *grown noticeably* under his *hand.* How often has he stood firm and upright *behind* his charges and, with great *penetration, entered* them…upon the road to manhood. Indeed I might add…

The PROFESSOR has been following the BISHOP's testimony with increasing distress. At last he interrupts and addresses the audience.

PROFESSOR: Perhaps I might interrupt for a moment before we get too far afield. For the record and the audience's information, the Reverend Edward James Hutch did indeed enjoy a sterling reputation among his confreres and, I believe, with good reason. He ably comforted, instructed, and provided religious counsel to the young men in his care. Many a young man has testified to the salutary influence of Reverend Hutch on his moral education and spiritual growth. In 1918, at the height of the influenza epidemic that was decimating the nation, Reverend Hutch went voluntarily to the naval base at Newport. At great peril to himself, he comforted the sick, eased the way of the dying, and wrote the necessary painful letters to the faraway bereaved. In the worst days of the epidemic, two hundred young men arrived at the naval hospital *each hour.* It is perhaps impossible to imagine such horror, and impossible to conceive of the bravery and devotion of such a man.

Does this absolve the Reverend Hutch? I wish only to point out that a man may practice a secret vice with one hand while sincerely serving God with the other. Further judgments, ladies and gentlemen, I leave to you.

Pause.

REVEREND: If I might interpose a word of thanks, Professor—

PROFESSOR: Please…don't mention it. Mr Haney?

JAMIE: Yes…ahem… So… Bishop Woollett, in your view would it be possible for Reverend Hutch to commit the crimes he is accused of?

CHUCK: Quite impossible, sir.

JAMIE: Thank you, your Excellency. That will be all.

THEO: Your Excellency–

CHUCK: *Hm?*

THEO: How well do you know Reverend Hutch?

CHUCK: I've known him since he–did I answer this question already?

PROFESSOR: This is the prosecuting attorney, your Excellency.

CHUCK: Oh. I see. Wasn't he here before?

PROFESSOR: Please just answer the question.

THEO: If I might rephrase it. Are you on intimate terms with Reverend Hutch?

CHUCK: (*Outraged.*) *Intimate?*

THEO: I mean, do you know him *well?*

CHUCK: I have known his professional reputation for many years and have had several contacts with him during that time.

THEO: But you are not close friends.

CHUCK: No, sir.

THEO: So you could not really say what Reverend Hutch might or might not do?

CHUCK: I can only say that, given his reputation among the clergy not only of the Episcopal Church but of other churches as well, it is inconceivable to me that Reverend Hutch could commit an immoral act.

THEO: But you do not know for certain that he did not do so?

CHUCK: No, sir.

THEO: Thank you, Bishop Woollett. That will be all.

The BISHOP leaves the stand.

JAMIE: Your honor, the defense would like to call Ezekiel Vole to the stand.

THEO: Mr *Vole*?

JAMIE: Yes.

THEO: You wish to cross-examine Mr Vole *now*?

JAMIE: (*Sweetly, standing very close to THEO.*) With the kind permission of the prosecuting attorney.

THEO: (*Stepping away angrily.*) This seems highly irregular, your honor.

PROFESSOR: I think Mr Haney is within his rights, Mr Chump. Mr Vole will approach the stand.

MR VOLE enters and takes the stand.

JAMIE: Mr Vole, you are an expert on perversion.

THEO: Objection!

JAMIE: I am only repeating the witness's earlier characterization of himself.

MR VOLE: I believe I indicated that I was an expert on perverts.

JAMIE: Can you describe to the court what you know about them?

MR VOLE: A pervert is a twisted, stunted creature who can only receive sexual pleasure through perverse, unnatural acts.

JAMIE: But what I want to know, Mr Vole, is perversion congenital? That is, are perverts born or made?

MR VOLE: It is my view, sir, that there's some of both. Some of these creatures are born that way, the way you might be born with a hump back or a harelip.

JAMIE: So they should be pitied?

MR VOLE: Pity, sir, is a mistaken attitude towards a dangerous criminal. For a pervert won't rest till he's made more perverts.

JAMIE: How does he do that?

MR VOLE: By luring them into unnatural practises.

JAMIE: Perversion, then, is contagious?

MR VOLE: In a manner of speaking. It is possible that once a young man acquires a taste for these pleasures, he might never enjoy normal sexual intercourse again.

JAMIE: Are these pleasures so much greater, then?

MR VOLE: From my own experience, I cannot say–

JAMIE: Of course not, Mr Vole.

MR VOLE: –I can only say that perversion is a trap into which many a young man has been enticed. Perversion has its own unholy allure.

JAMIE: So it is in the interests of a just society to prevent our young men from having any contact with these perverts.

MR VOLE: It is indeed, sir.

JAMIE: Why, then, Mr Vole, were young men of the United States Navy sent out, by you, to engage in those acts whose very commission, you have told us, taints and corrupts?

THEO: Objection!

MR VOLE: I'll answer that question! My men were instructed to detest and abhor such vice and to do only what was necessary in that way to obtain evidence against criminals!

JAMIE: Ah! I see. And it is with abhorrence, then, that they entered these dens of perversion?

MR VOLE: Yes, sir.

JAMIE: And with abhorrence that they made assignations?

MR VOLE: Yes, sir.

JAMIE: With abhorrence that they allowed themselves to be kissed?

MR VOLE: Yes, sir.

JAMIE: That they allowed their instruments to be fondled?

MR VOLE: Yes, sir.

JAMIE: That they allowed their instruments to be sucked?

MR VOLE: Yes, sir.

JAMIE: It is with abhorrence that they committed sodomy? That they committed buggery?

THEO: Objection! The witness has answered the question.

PROFESSOR: Sustained.

JAMIE: I see now, Mr Vole, that there is a great difference between common perversion and the acts your men committed.

MR VOLE: There is indeed, sir.

JAMIE: Now could you explain to the court, sir, what 'difference' there is between you and a common panderer?

THEO: Objection! Mr Vole is not on trial here!

JAMIE: (*Circling THEO; spitting the words at him.*) Your honor, my client stands accused of the most vile acts, acts the very mention of which taints the air of this courtroom. It is the duty of this court to inquire scrupulously into the moral character of his accusers. The men who have accused Reverend Hutch freely admit committing acts of the most unspeakable vice, acts which the Reverend himself has denied with vehemence and horror. Mr Vole here admits to instructing his men in the particulars of this vice, to telling them that any depraved act is sanctioned as long as it is committed with the proper 'abhorrence'. Is this the case then? Are these acts condoned, are they more palatable, are they less perverse when they are sufficiently abhorred by those who commit them?

THEO: (*Seizing JAMIE's lapels.*) You little motherfucker!

PROFESSOR: Gentlemen, please!

JAMIE: (*Freeing himself with dignity.*) I have no further questions for Mr Vole. The defense, your honor, rests.

PROFESSOR: Mr Chump, have you any further questions?

THEO: (*With a murderous look at JAMIE.*) No.

PROFESSOR: Then might we bring this weary pageant to a close with your final remarks to the jury?

THEO steps down right and addresses the audience. The following three speeches overlap, as noted below.

THEO: Gentlemen of the jury, vice is a hideous thing, a vile, disfiguring disease. Vice, left to fester, can only further corrupt the body of the state. It is your duty today to see that this festering sore is cauterized and closed. Do not be deceived by appearances. The defendant appears before you as a man of God, but we have seen that underneath he is a captain of vice. Do not, as Mr Shakespeare says, let 'the strong lance of Justice hurtless break', deflected by priestly robes. You have heard the testimony of these young men. How many young man have we not heard from? How many young men have been lured into vice and perversion by this subtle deceiver? How many more if we do not act today? Do not turn away, gentlemen, from the hideous face of vice, but confront it, condemn it, and punish it with all the fury that Justice places now at your disposal.

JAMIE comes downstage left at 'Do not be deceived' and addresses the audience. THEO's speech continues sotto voce.

JAMIE: Gentlemen of the jury, you have the right to ask yourselves, who is the menace to public morals in Newport, Rhode Island? Is it this man of God whose reputation, before this regrettable farce, shone with the modest pure light of a simple servant of Christ? Or is it this Mr Vole and his 'investigators', who tell us that, by committing acts of unspeakable vice, they hoped to free us from these vices? I cannot believe that there is a man among you who is not sure of the answer without needing a fraction of a moment to deliberate. We have heard terrible things in this courtroom. We have heard of depraved acts–degraded acts of perversion–committed not by the good Reverend, but by those who hoped to snare him in their net. I ask you now, gentlemen, to end this good man's exile in the land of suspicion and calumny and restore to him his rightful place of honor and good repute.

MR PUMPHREY comes downstage center on 'Mr Vole' and addresses the audience. JAMIE's speech continues sotto voce.

PETEY: The jury is out, ladies and gentlemen, but the verdict is in. Are you listening, Mr Roosevelt? Under your direct orders, seamen have been instructed in the most vile practices in order to entrap the innocent. Something is rotten in the United States Navy. Must we hesitate any longer before tracing its source up to the highest offices in the land? Even as the fate of the good Reverend Hutch hangs in the balance this afternoon, we may with decision, with courage, with high indignation, say to Secretary Roosevelt, 'Guilty, sir! Guilty as charged! You can no longer hide, Mr Roosevelt, from the searching light of Justice!'

The three men exit, and ROOSEVELT's office appears onstage with ROOSEVELT and his AIDE.

MICK: The verdict is in, sir. Innocent on all counts.

CHUCK: Thank God.

MICK: We're hardly out of the woods, Mr Roosevelt.

CHUCK: No, but at least my mother will stop calling. What news from the Senate?

MICK: They can hardly contain their glee, sir. They've sniffed blood and they're going in for the kill. I'm afraid it won't be pretty.

CHUCK: Why can't they just let it go? He's innocent, isn't he? It's over.

MICK: Republicans, sir.

CHUCK: Animals.

MICK: You've been asked to prepare a statement for the Committee.

CHUCK: Yes, yes, only not now. Is there an aspirin tablet in the house?

MICK: I'll find one directly, sir.

CHUCK: If you would be so good.

The AIDE starts to go, then turns.

MICK: Sir?

CHUCK: What?

MICK: Do you *believe* he's innocent?

CHUCK: Who?

MICK: Reverend Hutch.

CHUCK: Hutch? Good Lord no! Guilty as sin! I'm surprised at you, Simpson. Really I am. What has that got to do with anything?

The AIDE exits. The office disappears and the PROFESSOR appears in the YMCA restaurant. He is eating breakfast once again as the REVEREND passes by.

REVEREND: Professor! Good morning!

PROFESSOR: (*Rising.*) Ah, Reverend Hutch! Let me be— certainly not the first—but among the many to congratulate you on the successful outcome of your—

REVEREND: Quite! Yes, yes! I'm a new man today, Professor! Liberated! May I–?

PROFESSOR: Of course.

They both sit.

REVEREND: Yes, you have no idea what it is to be–

PROFESSOR: I can only imagine–

REVEREND: A terrible weight—

PROFESSOR: Dear me, yes.

REVEREND: Right off of my shoulders! (*To ELLA who approaches the table.*) Only coffee, dear. (*To the PROFESSOR.*) Yes, yes...

Pause.

PROFESSOR: And what will you do now, Reverend?

REVEREND: Hm?

PROFESSOR: Have you any plans?

REVEREND: Oh, *plans*! Yes! Hundreds! It's been felt, of course, among my superiors that—uh—due to the recent—uh—difficulties—with no imputation whatsoever to my *own* comportment—none whatsoever—that it might be best—for all concerned—well, if I made myself scarce for a bit.

PROFESSOR: I see.

REVEREND: So I have applied, and been assured of acceptance, for a position on an ocean liner.

PROFESSOR: An ocean liner?

REVEREND: You know. Shipboard services. Weddings. Comfort to the seasick.

PROFESSOR: How delightful.

REVEREND: Yes, I think I shall quite like it. I've always been drawn to—uh—to the sea, you know.

PROFESSOR: Hm.

REVEREND: (*With sudden rancor.*) My only regret is that I shall miss seeing that scoundrel Roosevelt scourged in the Senate!

PROFESSOR: Now, Reverend, we must forgive our enemies as we hope to be forgiven.

REVEREND: Yes, yes, you are wiser than I, Professor. But then (*Sadly.*) you haven't lived as long.

As the restaurant booth disappears, VERN, as SENATOR BULLROSE, appears at the head of a Senate Committee. It is made up of the Decoys and Fairies in senatorial drag.

VERN: The opinion of the Senate Naval Affairs Committee on the Newport Affair is rendered as follows:

That in Newport, Rhode Island, those conditions which often exist in the vicinity of a crowded naval base obtained: namely, the practice of nefarious vices by recruits whose moral character was not of the highest and by those attracted to a Navy town to ply their infamous trades.

That, while such conditions are a menace to the health and morale of sailors, the instruction of mere boys to go forth into Newport to allow immoral acts to be practiced upon them is utterly shocking to the American standard of morality.

That any government official who would give his imprimatur to such activities is absolutely indefensible and most severely to be condemned.

We, therefore, do condemn the entire investigation and those responsible for it.

We reserve our strongest censure for Secretary of the Navy Roosevelt, at whose door the greatest share of blame must lie. We also severely condemn Chief Machinist's Mate Ezekiel Vole and recommend his immediate discharge from his naval duties.

MR VOLE appears downstage right.

We further recommend that, owing to certain irregularities in the arrest, detainment, and trial of the sailors snared in the investigation, all sailors condemned by evidence gathered in the investigation be forthwith freed and dishonorably discharged from the Navy...

JAMIE appears upstage left, a knapsack over his shoulder. The committee disperses. As JAMIE begins to speak, MR VOLE freezes for a moment, then with what chilly dignity he can muster, he crosses and exits.

JAMIE: (*Viciously.*) Well, if it isn't Mr Vole! I guess they gave it to you good and rough, didn't they, Mr Vole? And you just bending over every which ways to please them! Well, they knew just where to stick it to you! Take it like a man, Mr Vole! Who knows, you might even learn to like it!

MR VOLE is gone, but the PROFESSOR has entered to witness the last of this scene.

PROFESSOR: Jamie?

JAMIE: Professor! Look at me! I'm a free man.

PROFESSOR: Congratulations!

JAMIE: Well, the Navy moves in mysterious ways, its wonders to perform.

PROFESSOR: Are you off somewhere?

JAMIE: Don't know, Professor. Don't have a job now, do I?

PROFESSOR: Then you're leaving us.

JAMIE: I aim to. Maybe take off for the West Coast, get a job on a freighter. Somewheres they don't know me.

PROFESSOR: Well, I guess this is good-bye.

JAMIE: Could be. I got a thing or two to settle before I go.

PROFESSOR: A thing to—

THEO appears downstage, also carrying a knapsack.

JAMIE: (*Looking at THEO.*) Yeah. I'll be seeing you around, Professor.

The PROFESSOR withdraws to the shadows at the front of the stage.

I was waiting for you.

THEO: You needn't've bothered.

JAMIE: Maybe not. But I did anyway. (*Beat.*) You going somewhere?

THEO: Maybe. Can't stay here, can I?

JAMIE: Nope. I'm going west.

THEO: (*Lighting a cigarette; without interest.*) Yeah?

JAMIE: Yeah. I am. Come with me.

THEO: Naw.

JAMIE: No? Don't you want to?

THEO approaches JAMIE and puts his hand on his chest.

THEO: The only thing I want to do with you is get you outta my way so's I can be on my way.

He shoves JAMIE roughly aside and steps past him.

JAMIE: Where're you going so fast, sailor?

THEO: I'm not a sailor now, am I? I don't got nothing now. Thanks to you.

JAMIE: God, you're stupid.

THEO: Don't call me that.

JAMIE: You're so stupid. How do you dress yourself in the morning?

THEO: I'm warning you—!

JAMIE: You think it's me done this to you? It's *them*! You think you spent the last six months in a prison? What do you think this is? It's just one big worldwide trap. But think about this. You coulda had me. All that time we was locked up in that place together, we coulda had each other—at least. Don't tell me you didn't think about it. Don't tell me you didn't think about me and the good times we useta have.

THEO: The only thing I thought about was what I was gonna do to you when I got out. If I was you, I wouldn't remind me.

76

JAMIE: Did you let people do things to you? Huh? In the showers? In the toilet? Don't tell me you didn't.

THEO: Ain't none o' your business what I done. But I'll tell you one thing, all I thought about is when I get out I'm gonna get me a woman. A *real* woman. Not some twisted freak prancing around pretending. God, you make me puke!

JAMIE: Who're you kidding? If it wasn't for me, you'd-a been with a woman? If it wasn't for me, you'd-a been giving blow jobs in the public johns!

THEO hits him.

Oh, good! Hit me! That's brave! That's smart!

THEO hits him again.

What're you trying to prove, big boy? What're you trying to hide?

THEO: (*Hitting him.*) Shut up!

JAMIE: I'm twisted, am I? I'm a freak? What about you?

THEO: (*Hitting him.*) *Shut up!*

JAMIE: Go on! Run off! Marry a pretty little wife! In six months you'll be begging some queen to suck your cock!

THEO: SHUT UP!! (*He hurls JAMIE to the ground and starts off.*)

JAMIE: (*Screaming after him; in tears.*) Go on! Run! Run away! You can't run from yourself! Don't you know that? You stupid fuck! You stupid, senseless, brainless fuck!

The PROFESSOR steps forward suddenly and shouts at THEO.

PROFESSOR: Wait! Stop!

Without seeming to have heard him, THEO stops. He raises his hands to his face and sways a moment. JAMIE is still heaped on the ground, sobbing. Slowly, THEO turns and walks over to JAMIE. He falls to his knees before him, then buries his head in JAMIE's lap. The PROFESSOR turns to the audience. Apologetically:

Because there must—mustn't there?—be hope.

DAVID FOLEY

JAMIE is heard murmuring softly to THEO as he strokes his hair.

Now, we all know in our bones that there is *something* in each of us that is eternal. But what, I begin to wonder? Mightn't it be just the wish to be free, which burns—well, hardly like a beacon in the night—more like the tail of a firefly blinking in and out, just out of reach, disappearing into the shadows of a summer night, then reappearing to remind us—of something that we've missed?

JAMIE: (*Throughout the following, he speaks at times to THEO and at times to the PROFESSOR.*) Hush now, baby. It's all right. It's all right.

PROFESSOR: Mightn't it be that wish, that little light, that saves us, that makes us most human and most divine?

JAMIE: Shhhh. Shhhh.

PROFESSOR: And when I say freedom, I don't mean the freedom to *do* or the freedom to *be*, but the freedom to *create*.

JAMIE: That's it, baby. I'm here. I'm here.

PROFESSOR: We are all of us given at birth, in life, a peculiar mismatched and unpromising bag of materials to work with.

JAMIE: Oh, don't I know it, honey.

PROFESSOR: And the glory of human existence, the glory of the artists and the poets and the prophets as well as the window cleaner and the chambermaid, has been to create from this rag and bone shop of the soul something of beauty and of sense.

JAMIE: Ain't no sense in the world, Professor...

PROFESSOR: ...but the sense we make. If we could rise above...

JAMIE: (*Sadly, mockingly, tenderly.*) Rise above...

PROFESSOR: The prison of the world...

JAMIE: The locks and keys and bars...

PROFESSOR: If we could rise into that airy, empyrean realm the poets direct us to....

JAMIE: Come with me, baby. You'll see. You'll see.

PROFESSOR: If we could learn that beauty, order is something we create...

JAMIE: From the wreckage...

PROFESSOR: From the gorgeous, whirling chaos...

JAMIE: From the scraps they leave us. From the craziness and the hurt...

PROFESSOR: Freedom is...

JAMIE: A hole in the fence. You tear yourself going through...

PROFESSOR: The risk is, yes, great, but if we could find it, seize it, hold it...

JAMIE: If we could do it, baby, if we could find a way...

PROFESSOR: ⎫⎧ What wonders we could make...

JAMIE: ⎭⎩ What a world we could make...just for us...

PROFESSOR: This frightens us, naturally...

JAMIE: Don't be scared, baby. Don't be scared...

PROFESSOR: Freedom is a burden...

JAMIE: A burning in your gut...

PROFESSOR: A madness...

JAMIE: A fury...

PROFESSOR: It is a duty that falls on us all, a duty not all of us choose to assume...

JAMIE: This is it. This is our chance...

PROFESSOR: The duty of each of us, each morning of our lives...

JAMIE: Oh, baby, if we was just brave enough, just strong enough…

PROFESSOR: ⎱⎰ To create the world anew…

JAMIE: We could make the world anew…

Pause.

PROFESSOR: (*As if suddenly coming to himself; to the audience.*) Good night!

He leaves the stage as the lights slowly go down on JAMIE and THEO.

The End.